Flowing In
Living Waters

A 21st Century Guide To Spiritual Gifts

by

Jesse Moreland

www.rdtalleybooks.com

Las Vegas, Nevada

The primary Holy Bible version referenced in this book is the King James Version, however, some verses may be paraphrased.

Cover Designed by Alex Cotton
https://www.ginisismg.com/

ISBN: 978-1-957294-19-3

R.D. Talley Books Publishing, LLC
4882 W. Lone Mountain Rd.
Las Vegas, Nevada 89130
www.rdtalleybooks.com

Contents

On Spiritual Gifts

One day, years ago, I arrived at the DMV to attempt to register my vehicle. I was only recently filled with the Holy Spirit and started with earnest conviction to spend a lot of time in prayer. My parents and siblings, up until that point, already concluded that I was going mad with religion. I was shut up in my room, sometimes for hours at a time, spending time with the Holy Spirit. That day, God did something to me that changed my entire view about spiritual things.

As I stood waiting in line, I noticed a man who appeared to be glowing. At first, it was very subtle, but the longer I sat the more it bothered me. Finally, I worked up the courage to speak to the gentleman and discovered that he was a fellow believer. This prompting, or what I'd like to call 'Holy Ghost outline', was my first lesson in what I would later understand to be spiritual discernment.

As you can imagine, as a young Christian, I was blown away. I had never seen the supernatural become this real to me and I made a mistake a lot of Christians make: I began to think a little too much of myself. Without guidance at a young age, I made some foolish mistakes and wasted a lot of time.

I am Elder and Teacher Jesse Moreland and I wrote this book as a guide to help you navigate your spiritual experiences. Sometimes, as a person growing in Christ, you will see things, hear things, and maybe even smell things that others won't. You will be cast aside as an oddity at times because of people's lack of understanding. I hope that, through careful prayer and study, I can give you the entire counsel of God on spiritual gifts, and not just a passing thought or slight commentary.

Some gifts take very careful study because they are barely mentioned in scripture. I feel God has graced me to write this book to help the teacher and the student maximize the gifts in their lives. The Bible says in Galatians 6:1, *"If a brother be overtaken in a fault, you who are spiritual restore such a one"*. We often struggle in our churches. We struggle with what is spiritual and what is carnal. We struggle with how to restore others, and even with how to restore ourselves.

My prayer of faith today is that through the teaching of the Holy Ghost, the oil of the anointing will grace and empower this book to help others. I pray that through the Holy Spirit, God will empower you and anoint you to complete your task in the Holy Ghost. I pray in the spirit that the scripture will come to pass that reads, *"And he gave some apostles, some prophets, some evangelists, pastors and teachers. For the perfecting of the saints, for the work of the ministry. For the edifying of the body of Christ"* (Ephesians 4:11-12). I hope that this book will build and edify you.

For the past year, God has given me a burning desire to expound on every gift. If you haven't experienced a gift, I hope to bring you testimonies of people who have. I hope that when I'm finished, you will have a full understanding of what God has called you to do and the tools God has given you. I hope you won't skip over chapters in this book on integrity, because I want you to know that a clean heart is more important than a gift.

Remember 1 Corinthians 13:1; if you don't have love, these gifts profit you nothing. I want you to know the importance of divine order and that these gifts are given for the body of Christ. A tree cannot eat its own fruit. With these things in mind, I would like you to join me on this journey of spiritual growth and maturity.

I want to thank the leaders who believe in me and that have given me every opportunity for my gifts to grow and flourish. Teachers are not accepted in every place, so once again, my love and appreciation.

I would like to give special thanks to Pastor Latina Reagan, whose love and attention to detail has helped me grow.

I want to thank Overseer Davidson, who's covering and guidance has kept me through the years. She is a true mother to me in the spirit.

I want to thank the late-Pastor Aron Davidson, who is the best definition of a friend that I could think of. I love and miss you Pastor Aron and can't wait to see you in heaven.

I want to thank Apostle Albert Davidson, who fathered me in the faith. A man who spoke destiny and purpose into my life, and laid hands on me imparting things into me. I wish the world had more spiritual fathers.

I want to thank Apostle Carl Maze, a wise old man with whom I've spent countless hours sitting near, listening to him expound on God's word. I pray to God that when I I'm old and gray that I can pass on the things I have learned and mentor others.

And lastly, I want to give special thanks to my wife Sharon, who is one of the most insightful people I have ever met. A woman who will always push me to excellence. I love you dear. I pray that this book will indeed be living water to you. I pray that it will unlock things in you springing up into a wellspring of life.

1

Prophetic Integrity, Definitions and Guidance

The first thing I want to address is the state of your salvation. Have you been saved? Are you walking in a place of sanctification? If you're picking up this book then you are looking in the right place, but if you're not sure you are saved, I want you to pray this prayer with me out loud:

Father God, in the name of Jesus, you said in your word that if I would confess with my mouth the Lord Jesus and believe in my heart that God raised him from the dead, I would be saved. God, I come before you today confessing that Jesus died for me, and that you raised him up on the third day. I repent and turn away from all my sins. I renounce them and I accept your salvation on this day. In Jesus name, Amen.

Friends, if you have prayed this prayer with me, I want you to know that you are saved TODAY! The Bible says the angels in heaven are rejoicing! There is contact information in this book for my home church, Cornerstone Family and Worship. I am currently sitting under Pastor Latina Reagan and we would love to have you come visit us or join us online. Now that you are saved, you need to be around a spirit-filled church that will help you grow.

The second thing I want to address is the baptism of the Holy Spirit. There is more than one baptism: there is baptism in water, but also a baptism in the spirit (Acts 1:5 and Acts 19:2). When the Holy Ghost fell on them on the day of Pentecost, this was the baptism in the spirit.

Receiving the Holy Ghost baptism can happen to you in several ways. In fact, I want you to pray this prayer with me right now if you aren't filled. We are going to pray that God would fill you with the spirit. Pray this prayer with me:

Father God, in the name of Jesus, you said in your word, in Acts Chapter 1 verse 8, that I would receive power after the Holy Ghost has come upon me. God, I ask for the power of your spirit to overshadow me right now. God fall on me, dwell in me, and fill me with your spirit. I believe your word on today. In Jesus' name, Amen.

Friends if you have said this prayer, I'm looking for you to testify that you had a Holy Ghost encounter. I'm waiting to hear your testimonies that God overshadowed you, and that you spoke with tongues or prophesied like the Bible says. I'm looking forward to seeing you grow in the Lord.

The third thing I want to address is the concept of prophetic integrity. When I say prophetic, I'm using the term as a blanket word, or in reference to anything insightful in the word or the spirit of God. The Word 'prophet', or 'prophetic', means someone who speaks as an oracle or a mouthpiece for God. The word 'integrity' refers to your honesty and upright dealings. We are going to use the definition like this.

Prophetic Integrity: keeping the office, position, or platform that you hold spiritually, in a manner that glorifies God, is honest before men and God, submits to correction and authority, and that doesn't give you a guilty conscience.

"Cleanse yourself from all filthiness of the flesh and spirit, and perfect holiness in the fear of the Lord." (2 Corinthians 7:1)

"Thou I speak with the tongues of men and of angels and have not love." (1 Corinthians 13:1)

"Didn't we cast out devils in your name, and prophesy in your name?" (Matthew 7:22)

Here are rules to live by that will allow you to keep your integrity while you grow in God. Here are some tips to remember on prophetic integrity:

1. If you're going to walk in spiritual gifts, they are for the building or edifying of the body of Christ.
2. Spiritual gifts are never to be used for monetary profit, i.e. giving the word of knowledge for money. (Acts 8:18-20)
3. No one operating under the leading of the Holy Spirit will call Jesus cursed, deny Jesus nor deny his God-head (That is his deity). (1 John 4:2 & 4:15, 1 John 5:1 & 5:11, 1 Corinthians 12:3)
4. The spirit of the prophet, or speaker, is subject to the speaker. You have control over your body and tongue. You make the choice to speak and to stop speaking. (1 Corinthians 14:32)
5. Just because you operate in a spiritual gift, it doesn't mean that you're righteous. (1 Corinthians 13:1 & Romans 11:29)
6. Just because you have a gift, it doesn't mean that you aren't subject to authority. (Romans 13:1 & 1 Corinthians 14:29)

Let every soul be subject to the higher power.

This is a major issue with people as they grow and develop in gifts and callings. The Bible discusses being subject to the governing authorities. Most people typically translate this scripture to mean the world and its government, but God has set up the church in the earth as a governing body over spiritual things (1 Corinthians 6:2, 1 Corinthians 5:3-13, 1 Corinthians 14:29).

The church was designed to judge spirits and to judge the affairs of the church, not judge the world. If you read carefully, God, speaking through Apostle Paul, even gave the church authority to cast out the individual who brought shame on the church. For some reason, the government of the church is a hard concept for people to deal with. Even when Jesus said judge ye not, he was talking mostly about hunting and judging unrighteously (Matthew 7:1). I could write another book on the government of the church, but for time's sake I am just going to share a few things. We will use the scripture starting at Romans 13:1-3:

"Let every soul be subject to the higher power". If God allows unrighteous men to set up government for the benefit of mankind, then why wouldn't he set up church government? We will therefore conclude that even if you don't agree with your pastor or bishop being in authority, there is a divine purpose and reason for him being there.

"For there is no power but of God, and the powers that be are ordained of God". Believe it or not, everything that God made has been given a place, a power and an authority. Even the devil has been given a power and authority for a time (Luke 4:6). The Church's authority is

to judge and govern spiritual things, to judge spirits as we have mentioned earlier. The word 'discern' means to perceive or recognize something, leading to judge. Now, I don't mean the kind of judgment that's cruel, critical, and heartless, but the kind of judgment that tells the truth and restores.

The Bible says if a brother is overtaken in a fault, you who are spiritual must restore him. The church has been given the ability to put out and restore. What we are discussing here is righteous judgment. Jesus talks about how if you're going to judge, then judge righteously. The word is truth. If you're going to give people the word, then the word itself will judge. Matthew 7:1 says, *"Judge ye not lest you be not judged"*. Here, He is discussing unrighteous judgment. Notice He says, "with the same judgment you use, it shall be measured back". So, if I'm sinning and in error, then yes, I want someone to tell me the truth in righteousness judgment. If my words are true, then I want the church to be able to discern the difference (Hebrews 5:14).

We are getting into a spiritual law here, but I want you to understand that with the same measure of judgment you use, it will be measured back. If you're cruel and evil, then expect the same. If you're truthful and righteous, then expect the same. I'm teaching this because I want the church to be free from the religion of thinking that you can't correct a brother in error. I want the church to have a Godly reverence for the God in each other, and know that if you're cruel, then the same cruelty will be measured.

"Whoever resisteth the power resisteth the ordinance of God". So, when you resist the governing authorities, you resist the order of God. Now, brothers and

sisters, I am not writing this to say that you should just accept abuse or allow for a pastor to do evil. There are ways of handling this. I'm trying to tell you that the church has been given government and authority by God. If you're going to leave a church, there is a right way and a wrong way to leave. If you have an accusation against a leader, there is a right and wrong way to address the situation. Even if you have a house church, then someone has been given that vision, and someone must lead. You would have anarchy in the world's system with no form of governance. Why would the church be any different? To make matters worse, spirits tend to run wild where there is no governing authority or person to police things (1 Timothy 5:19).

"And they that resist shall receive in themselves damnation". Again, the church was never designed to have every member separated. The Bible speaks about forsaking to assemble yourselves. The church was designed to be a body with a head. If you don't stay attached to the body, that's called division.

"For rulers are not a terror to good works but to evil". A good ruler will be a terror to evil works. Once again, your man or woman of God has been given spiritual authority, to both restore and to put away. Don't allow your gift to make you puffed up! (1 Timothy 3:6)

I've put together a simple acronym that will keep you honest during your journey. Keep it in mind, it will help you stay integral. Our acronym today is ICEPOP. I know it sounds simple, or even childish, but please bear with me. I pray that the Holy Spirit will remind you of these things when you are tempted.

'I' stands for *integrity*. Remember, when a man's ways please the Lord, he gives you favor with God and man. It's very difficult to be hated (because of your own evils, not the gospel) and minister at the same time.

'C' stands for *conscience*. We discovered in Hebrews 9:12-14 that you need your conscience purged to really serve God. In other words, if you're constantly under a guilt trip, it will hinder you. No, this doesn't mean do evil and ignore your conscience. It doesn't mean pretend that you didn't hurt others. It means that when you have messed up, you repent and move forward. What good does it do to ask for God's forgiveness if you don't accept it?

Keep in mind that the devil is an accuser. Have you ever done something wrong, and as soon as you enter church or worship, your enemy the devil flashes things across your mind that you did? Or makes you feel unworthy? It's your job to cast down imaginations and evil thoughts. It's easier to not do things that affect your conscious than to struggle with this. Keep a clear conscience. It will help you.

'E' stands for *edify*. Remember that your sole purpose for asking God to use you in these gifts is to build up the body of Christ. They are not here to make you money, (the lust of the eyes) or make your selfish desires come true (the lust of the flesh). They are not here to make you look good (the pride of life). These are all things that are a trap and a snare.

The devil has used the same playbook from the beginning. Remember, words are spirits. When the devil approached Jesus, he didn't wear a suit. He didn't approach him as a giant beast. He simply approached him with words

(Matthew 4:3). *"If you are the son of God turn these stones to bread."* In other words, use your abilities, Jesus, to feed your appetite. Use your abilities to show people who you are rather than edify.

'P' stands for *prayerful*. Looking for a shortcut is another trap and snare. I have news for you: there are no shortcuts in the kingdom of God. When Jesus said, *"these kinds only come out by prayer and fasting"* (Matthew 17:21), he means it. There is no Godly shortcut or revelation that will make you a walking wonder. Just like in a marriage, there is no fast shortcut to a solid relationship. Those who seek a shortcut rather than put in the work are destined to fail or live in mediocrity.

I'm not saying work as in something strenuous or harsh. Notice how when Adam was in the garden, he had plenty to do. He had to tend to the garden and keep it. He had to name all the animals, and whatever he called them, God backed him up. During this time, he was in the garden fulfilling his purpose. He had a lifetime of work to do, but if he walked with God, it was easy. Adam got kicked out. Now all he had to do was feed his family, except now it was hard. When you're walking with God, true relationship and prayer is easy. Your mindset shouldn't be on shortcuts.

'O' stands for *overcoming*. Paul talks about how because of the abundance of revelations, a thorn in his side was given to him; a messenger of Satan to buffet him (2 Corinthians 12:7). You must keep in mind that as you begin to grow, God will allow certain things to challenge you. I could write another book simply dealing with the challenges that each calling must face, and the grace that's needed to survive them. I'm going to simply tell you that

God will never tempt or challenge you above what you can bear.

The challenge is not in your life to break you, but to build and edify you. Giving up doesn't make the challenge go away. We can't simply wish our thorns away. Most of the time, if God put it there, you can't even pray it away. You must simply overcome it. At times, you may need to outlast the trial. Overcoming may mean that you grow to a place where it's a distant memory. But you must recognize that issues that are part of your process, you can't run from them. You must deal with them head-on. We will talk later about what challenges are typical of every ministry in the five-fold.

'P' stands for *persistent*. If you're going to be prayerful, don't pray and then stop. If you're going to fast, build a routine. The scripture talks about praying without ceasing. Remember, think of your body as a slave. A better modern-day illustration would be a robot. You must program your body to do whatever it is you want it to do. This is what Paul means when he writes about disciplining his body and bringing it into subjection.

The key to being persistent is discipline and training. If you want persistent prayer, then discipline or program your body to pray at a certain time on a certain day. I remember that I used to have a prayer time at 10:00pm every night at my old job. Some nights, I would forget to pray but find myself humming a worship song I couldn't get out of my head. Even though my mind had forgotten, my body was in the mood to pray because that's what I trained it to do.

This works the opposite way also. If you train your body to go to sleep whenever you read or pray, then you will develop bad habits. This is why when a smoker first starts smoking, the body quickly rejects it. After a while, the body not only adjusts, but builds up an addiction to it. If your body can build up a habit for cigarettes or falling asleep, then it can build up a habit to worship and pray. Persistence is key. Even the secular world will tell you if you do the same thing for about a month, it will become habit.

REMEMBER, YOU ARE TRAINING YOUR FLESH TO
DO SPIRITUAL THINGS!

Ways In Which God Speaks To You In The Spirit

God does speak through other means, like divine providence, other preachers and believers, and some testify that He has spoken to them audibly. But how does God speak to most of us individually? Remember, God will never tell you to do something outside of his word.

We have read in another place that no one that curses Jesus, or denies Jesus, is speaking by the spirit of God. When I say deny, I'm not just talking about his existence, but denying his deity and his God-head (1 Corinthians 12:3, Colossians 2:8, 1 John 2:22). The word 'Christ' means the anointed one (Hebrews 1:8-9).

Impressions. This is when you feel like God is encouraging you to say something. Sometimes it can be a gentle nudge, or at other times a nagging impression. Sometimes, it can feel like a pulling on your heartstrings.

Sometimes, it will be strong enough to feel like it's just bubbling up out of you.

Inner Voice. This is the inner voice or the still small voice that many people refer to. As you grow in God you will begin to distinguish your inner voice from the voice of God. This is just one of the ways, however, that God speaks to you. Therefore, it's important to understand what gates or avenues that God speak through. There are exercises in this book that will help you to see and understand the different ways in which God talks to you. At times, with the gift of tongues and interpretation, you will hear tongues with your inner voice. You will be encouraged to speak what you hear.

Visions. At times, you will see things happening. It will start out faintly but then begin to grow as you progress.

Feeling Infirmities or Body Impressions. This is common with the gift of discernment. You will feel other people's pain or infirmities so that you can minister to them.

Open Visions. People very strong in the prophetic gift will often have trance-like visions. They will go and visit places or see things in the spirit. If you don't believe me, just turn to the book of Revelations.

Holy Spirit Outlines. This can sometimes seem like a vision where the spirit will outline certain things. I have had this happen when studying scripture, as I've mentioned before in this book.

This Holy Spirit will outline for me a passage of scripture that He wants me to study or talk about. He will outline a person in the room to single out.

Thoughts. Like we mentioned in other places, when God speaks through your thoughts, it's normally disruptive to your thought process. Sometimes he's dealing with us through our thoughts, and we fail to act on them because it feels like our thoughts. We forget that the spirit is dwelling in us.

His Written Word, or bringing his word back to your remembrance (John 14:26).

Problems People Face When Flowing In The Gifts

Why do I feel weaker after I minister? There is a portion of scripture where Jesus is surrounded by people. Luke 8:42-46 reads, *"for he had an only daughter about twelve years of age, and she was dying. But as He went, the multitudes thronged Him. And a woman having an issue of blood twelve years, which had spent all her living upon physicians, neither could be healed of any, came behind him, and touched the border of his garment: and immediately her issue of blood stanched. And Jesus said, who touched me? When all denied, Peter and they that were with him said, Master, the multitude throng thee and press thee, and sayest thou, who touched me? And Jesus said, somebody hath touched me: for I perceive that virtue is gone out of me."* The power in Jesus is the power of the Holy Spirit. It is the anointing of God. There are a few principles to understand here.

You must understand that Jesus is the word made flesh, and we are flesh being made into the word. If some random woman can pull the anointing from Jesus, then the same can happen to us. Faith is one of the most powerful forces in the universe because faith can move the hand of God. Faith can cause virtue to flow. This is why after ministering you must restore yourself; you must replenish the virtue.

Remember, God is infinite, but you are God-dependent. You are poor in spirit (Matthew 5:2). Therefore, when people pull from the God in you, it must be restored. Think of your body and spirit as a well (John 7:38). What makes the well flow is your faith! Whether it's your faith or another person's faith, wherever there is true faith, the spirit of God will flow.

How do I restore myself? You must put back the virtue and power that was given out by spending time with God. The word says this in Acts 3:19; *"Repent ye therefore, and be converted, that your sins may be blotted out, when the times of refreshing shall come from the presence of the Lord;"*.

What you must know is that God has a word and a time of refreshing in his presence for you. Therefore, it's extremely important to be alone after you minister. Do not let people touch you when you're done or talk to you about problems or nonsense. I'm not saying this to be anti-social, but you're guarding your heart. If you feel tiredness, impatience or weaker after ministry, it's because virtue has gone out. Get in God's presence.

How do I turn it on? If you're asking how to be activated in the spirit, the answer is simple. Everything works by faith. Galatians 3:5 talks about the spirit working by the hearing of faith. If you're looking to be activated, the first step is knowing what God has for you. Faith comes by hearing and hearing comes by the word of God. That's why I want you to read this and search the scriptures. Meditate, think on these things, and declare these scriptures to yourself (2 Corinthians 4:13).

Whatever you believe, you must speak. I want to go deeper into faith later, but for now, I want you to understand and know, not just about faith, but how God has made you. What are your triggers? Some people can study the word and the Holy Spirit will move on them. Some people worship. Some hear tongues and immediately the spirit moves. You must know who you are in God.

In 2 Kings 3:15, there is a prophet that requests that a musician come before him before he prophesies. What I am explaining here is that God wants you to act in a level of intentional activation. More on this later.

Also, you must understand that the spirit of the prophet is subject to the prophet (1 Corinthians 14:32). This means that you are in control of your own spirit! When you pray in tongues, your spirit prays. You're speaking as the spirit GIVES the utterance. The only way that your tongues are fake is if they are not spoken in faith. You open your mouth and the spirit gives it the substance. This is an issue many Christians face. Your tongues don't have to be perfect because you're speaking by faith.

Another reason why we are not activated in the spirit is because we don't ask. The Bible says we have not because we ask not (James 4:3). The Bible says that we should earnestly desire the best gifts (1 Corinthians 14:1).

Many times, we have the wrong attitudes about ourselves and others, so our sense of low self-worth hinders our faith. We also ask amiss so that we can spend it on pleasures. Remember, your gifts are for the edification of the body of Christ and not for monetary or personal gain. The Holy Spirit will use the gifts to guide you in business, but we cannot sell the anointing. We are not soothsayers, witches or people that prostitute our gifts. Freely we have received, freely we give. I didn't say that you could never accept an offering. Accepting an offering is different than using your gifts for selfish gain (1 Corinthians 14:12). If you desire to be activated, ask in faith, not doubting and expect an answer (James 1:5).

Think of the Holy Spirit as a radio station. God is always thinking of you. Hebrews 2:6 says that God is mindful of you, so your spirit man is like the radio dial on the station. God's thoughts are flowing but you MUST be on the correct channel to be active. All these things like faith, attitude, knowing what triggers you, and asking will put you on the correct channel. I was surprised to discover that when I was on the correct channel, I didn't always get a word of knowledge, or some prophecy. I was surprised when God would give me a lesson in scripture, or even practical advice and ideas. The key is getting in the spirit. The common denominator to all the things I mentioned as triggers is getting in the spirit. You worship in the spirit, pray in the spirit, and even study to show yourself approved in the spirit.

How do I turn it off? Some people have this issue of not being able to find rest when they begin flowing in the spirit. They are constantly seeing things or are filled with revelations. Remember, the spirits of the prophets are subject to the prophets. It's important for your spirit man to rest just like your flesh rests. When I say rest, I don't mean to sleep, but a spirit-rest, just like God did. Hebrews 4:9-10 talks about a rest in the spirit for God's people. Note that this rest is not talking about death because the scripture talks about entering rest on earth. It's not a day because the Sabbath wasn't enough according to Hebrews. Your spirit man rests when it's not speaking and creating, just like God did.

When God worked, he spoke. When your spirit man works, its speaking. Yes, it is God speaking through you, but he's using your spirit man. So, rest is when you're not working in the spirit. If you are having an abundance of revelations, ask God to allow your spirit rest and then spend quiet time with him being replenished and restored. During this time, cease from ministry, unless you're given instructions. Remember, as we discussed, people can pull from you, so it's important if you want rest to avoid some people's conversations and issues. This is the primary reason why people that are real prophets tend to be introverted.

Remember, as we discussed before, there is a time of refreshing that comes from the Lord (Acts 3:19). Think about it: if God rested, shouldn't every other spirit need rest? Notice how even devils seek rest! (Matthew 12:43). Allow your spirit to rest. Allow God to refresh you.

What does it mean when I feel pushing or pulling? Now remember, we talked earlier about the woman with an issue of blood. Luke 8:42-45 talks about how the woman touched Jesus and virtue went out of him. She received a healing because of her faith, but healing is just one gift.

What about prophecy, or word of knowledge? If a healing can be wrought by faith, then what about the other gifts? We will discuss faith more in the next chapter, but here we see an important principle. The gifts of the spirit are activated and operate through faith in God. He even said in an important place in scripture, *"And these signs will follow them that believe"* (Mark 16:17). You are going to operate according to where you are in your faith process.

We see another principle in operation also. Faith is so powerful that it will cause the hand of God to move, no matter who has the faith. If another person can believe to the degree that they suck healing from Jesus, then all the other gifts apply. Here are some things to help you understand what's going on.

A. There will sometimes be a pull when you're ministering where people's faith will pull the anointing from you. I have seen my best teaching with people that are hungry. Hunger and desire can help develop faith, and the need and desire will cause a flow to happen. Some people call this a pull to prophecy. I like to call it a push to avoid confusion. You will feel in the spirit the Holy Ghost flowing and a solid flow.

B. There is a negative pull, almost like a wall, when you're ministering and people either don't understand or don't believe. If people feel like they already know, or don't receive you, you can feel it. This is why discernment is so important in the body of Christ. And not discerning by instinct or environment, but true discernment in the spirit.

C. The problem is not always people pulling at you when you're ministering. The problem is also people pulling at you when the flow of the spirit is over. This is the reason true prophets can be very reclusive. God might be done speaking for the night, and if you let them, people will pull at you. You never want to prophecy if God is done. You need to ask God when to release things, and when not to. To make matters worse, you must understand that discernment is a gift that is almost always on to some degree. So even if God is done speaking in the prophetic, you can still pick people up. Again, this is a good reason to take time alone after ministry. Never get tempted to prophecy if God has instructed you to finish up. When the Holy Ghost is done, He's done. This is one of the reason some ministers hit and miss.

Hitting and Missing

Now, I have heard a wide variety of things on the subject. Some leaders are very liberal and will gladly allow people to practice on their members. Some are very lenient with prophetic mess-ups. Others are very strict to the point that they will censor you for a slight mistake. The answer in my humble opinion is somewhere in between. I am not comfortable with someone exercising over God's people without supervision. At the same time, fear can discourage people from speaking up. I truly believe that if a person is not hearing God correctly, then they need to understand how to hear the voice of God and discover what is hindering them. If you do mess up, please repent and start fresh. If you have led someone down a path that has caused damage, repent. Ask your leaders how to be restored and renewed if you have made a mistake.

I will never forget that when I was first saved, I would bump into ministers all the time who would get things completely wrong. I was always told, "Thus saith the Lord, stop hanging around the wrong crowd", or "you have to get right with God", when all I did was lay on my face and pray. Is getting a prophecy wrong ok? Certainly not! At the same time, if you're missing a lot, I hope this book helps you get back on track. Here are some of the reasons people don't hear God correctly and how to fix it.

1. Unrepentant sin in your life. We have all missed the mark before. But remember, as we discussed before, you must walk in a place where you are confident that God hears you. I will tell you a secret about God that many will refuse to believe. Are you ready? God doesn't listen much to sinners. In fact, he hides his face from them (Isaiah 1:13-15). You cannot be a sinner and God's prophet at the same time.

In order to really flow in God, you need two-way communication. Sin separates you from God. But if you are walking with God, and have dealt with your sin, you are not a sinner. A sinner practices sin. A saint doesn't. Just like an ice skater will practice skating, or a driver practice driving, a sinner practices sin. A Christian practices Christ. Getting a hold of sin in your life and dealing with yourself is the first step in hearing clearly.

2. Emotional connections. Sometimes when a person is close to you, you end up telling them what they want to hear. It's very easy to get close to someone emotionally and end up saying what they want to hear to make them feel better rather than telling them what God says. This is why it can be awkward for close family members to minister to each other. You know all each other's business, so it can be difficult to be objective, or tell them no. We must mature to the place that if God said it, that settles it.

We always must be careful to not prophecy things out of anger or frustration. Just because we are angry at a person doesn't mean that God is angry. We are people with emotions and not emotional people. I would be wary of anyone that says they discern something when they are angry or offended. God is not in your anger. That's intuition. Also, never get in a place where you feel the need to prove anything. God doesn't work in this way. We are not fortune tellers.

3. Looking for voices. Remember, if you are looking for audible voices, you will likely find one. But just because you find a voice doesn't mean that you found the voice of God. The Holy Spirit's job is to teach you things and bring things the word has said to your remembrance (John 14:26). If you're seeking to hear from God, you must know what He will say, and what He won't. How God will say things, and how he won't. Can God speak to you in an audible voice? Yes. Will He most of the time? No.

4. Allowing your desire to speak louder than God's voice. This one can be huge, especially if you're seeking to be married. This is why I would encourage any couple that's seeking marriage to get a lot of counseling. The councilor might notice many things that you don't see. It is very easy to slip up and make a mistake because of desire rather than God's guidance.

5. Allowing your spiritual ears to grow dull or sleep. You can start out well, but then refuse to have a prayer life over the next ten years and falter. This is the problem with the people I mentioned earlier. They likely started off fresh with a fresh filling of the Holy Ghost. But as time progressed, they didn't water the seed. They didn't feed it what it needs. Their spiritual ears and eyes became dull. Their seed became dormant, or sleep. And instead of prophesying with fresh oil, they now rely on intuition. But remember, God sees differently than man sees.

The Bible says this: *"Blessed is the man that walketh not in the counsel of the ungodly, nor standeth in the way of sinners, nor sitteth in the seat of the scornful. But his delight is in the law of the Lord; and in his law doth he meditate day and night. And he shall be like a tree planted by the rivers of water, that bringeth forth fruit in its season; his leaf also shall not wither; and whatsoever he doeth shall prosper."* (Psalms 1:1-3). Now let's examine this:

"Blessed is the man who walks not in the council of the ungodly": So here is the part where God wants you to order your thoughts. He wants you to order what information that you take in and feed your spirit with. He doesn't want you to behave like a sinner or a scorner (someone that trash talks, sneers or has disdain for others).

"But his delight is in the law of the Lord": As you delight yourself in him, God will give you your desires.

"and in his law doth he meditate day and night": Again, if you want to hear God clearly, you must put your thinking in order. With no faith, God has nothing to work with. And with no word in you, you can't have faith because faith comes by hearing, and hearing by the word of God. If you don't feel like God hears you when you pray, or if you don't believe that God will answer you, you're not ready.

29

"And he shall be like a tree planted": This means you have taken the seed, which is your faith, and planted it. You have planted it where it can grow and become strong. It has nothing choking the seed.

"by the river of waters": This means you planted your seed in a place where there is a flow of the spirit. If you don't keep your seed near the flow of God, it will dry up.

"that bringeth forth fruit in its season": These actions cause fruit to spring up and reproduce fruit. You don't just have joy, you reproduce joy. You don't just have gifts, you reproduce gifting. Others come to you to eat and be nurtured. Remember, a tree cannot eat its own fruit, but every tree must reproduce of its own kind.

"his leaf also shall not wither": The leaves are for healing. Remember, you are a healthy tree (Galatians 5:22, Revelation 22:1).

"And whatsoever he doeth shall prosper."

Knowing Your Triggers

I want to talk briefly about not just knowing who you are in the spirit, but knowing how God uses you. Depending on your vocation and call, some things may cause you to be stirred. Prophets can be extremely sensitive to atmosphere. In fact, as mentioned before, there is a scripture in the Bible where the prophet called for soft music to be played before the answer came.

Teachers, on the other hand, can be instantly triggered by information or a revelation. Some people don't need to be triggered at all. They can go right in. Knowing how you flow can be very important. You may be triggered in the spirit by worship, praise, just hearing the word, or tongues. Some people are fiery and can operate with a lot of activity and noise. Some people cannot.

The Power of A Breakthrough

This word 'breakthrough' is a mystery to many people. It's not mentioned in the Bible in many places and it is seldomly understood. In this section, I will try to help you understand the importance of a breakthrough and the power of it.

We must understand that the Holy Spirit is infinite, but we are finite. The Holy Spirit is the living water, and we are the well. Therefore, we are not infinite in our ability to operate in the Holy Ghost. Remember, when God is done speaking, He is done. If we endeavor to stay in the realm of the prophetic permanently, then we will have trouble relating to others. Furthermore, we must keep in mind that the gifts are given for the edifying of the body of Christ, and not for selfish gain.

We talked earlier about how Jesus could feel virtue leave out of him. God wants to be our source. The cycle of giving out and being refilled is called breakthrough. Here are some scriptures that will help you.

Acts 5:31 is proof enough that you can be filled with the Holy Spirit more than once. In fact, you should look forward to it and expect that every time you pray and ask him to move for you, he will fill you.

Now, this doesn't mean that you are not saved, or that God is not with you, but this fresh infilling is one of the ways in which God the Holy Spirit bears witness with your spirit that He is there (Romans 8:16). Here are a few definitions for breakthrough. Keep in mind they all apply to help you understand.

A. A breakthrough is a military term for a military victory. It usually involves success in breaking an enemy's control of an area.
B. A breakthrough is a term used in science, which tells others that you have made a discovery in a specific field.
C. A term used for an epiphany, or an insight.

So, when you talk about a breakthrough, any one of the definitions will fit. A breakthrough is when you have an epiphany or realization that you have heard from God, and God has heard from you. A breakthrough is when you know in your heart that you have touched the heart of God and God has touched you. A breakthrough is when you know that a God has heard your cries and that deliverance has taken place. The Bible talks about how an angel was sent to Daniel, and that God heard him as soon as he prayed, but a prince (demon or principality) hindered the message. The angel had to breakthrough to Daniel (Daniel 10:12-14). The angel came to bring understanding. If we have things we struggle with, does it hinder our flow and understanding?

You should seek to be filled with a fresh out pour daily. It doesn't mean that you don't have the spirit. Receiving a breakthrough means that you have received fresh understanding, fresh anointing and fresh fire. He wants you to seek him and hunger for him daily.

Let's us pray and ask God for breakthrough today! Please pray out loud with me:

Father God, in Jesus' name we pray. God, we declare your word over our lives. Fill us with the fresh fire of your anointing. Strengthen us in this hour. Give us breakthrough into the heavens God. You promised you would pour out your spirit on all flesh and we believe it on today. Change our lives, as we yield to you. In Jesus name, amen.

Teaching Guide

What does it mean to let every soul be subject to the higher power?

Where is this found in scripture?

Why is it important to have prophetic integrity?

What does 1 John 4:2 tell us about people speaking by the spirit of God?

Give us a full definition of prophetic integrity as mentioned in the chapter.

What was the acronym we used to help you to remember integrity?

What are 3 problems that people face while flowing in the spirit?

1.

2.

3.

And what are the solutions?

1.

2.

3.

2

Prophesy According To Your Faith!

(Mark 4:30, Luke 14:19, Matthew 17:15-20)

There is a peculiar scripture in the Bible that says, *"Having then gifts differing according to the grace that is given to us, whether prophecy, let us prophesy according to the proportion of faith; (Romans 12:6)."* Now, my brothers and sisters, what does this mean? Does this mean we just say whatever and have faith that it comes to pass? Does this mean if we concentrate and believe really hard, something will happen? In this chapter we will discuss faith principles to help you understand the things of the spirit.

The first thing we must understand is that there are different levels of faith, just like there are different levels of operation in the spirit. There are:

A. **Saving Faith**: Faith in Jesus Christ. Faith that He died for you on the cross and that you're saved through grace. (Romans 10:9)

B. **Little Faith**: Faith that will go out, in ministry, and even operate in the spirit. But that can't get certain tasks done.

C. **Seed Faith**: This is the systematic faith that Jesus talks about in the scriptures. This is systematic faith. It is understanding the faith process.

D. **Most Holy Faith**: This is the faith that brings us behind the veil and into the most holy place. More on that later.

In this chapter, I want to discuss seed faith and seed faith principles. Seed faith is the process in which you activate biblical principles through the process of sowing and reaping. So, everything you do for God, I want you to look at as seed. Think about it for a moment: usually when God is explaining concepts of the kingdom, he uses the analogy of seedtime and harvest. (Genesis 8:22)

A. When you sow money into the kingdom, you release your faith with your money. Malachi 3:11 talks about not allowing the enemy to destroy the fruit of your ground.
B. You can sow into your flesh or sow into the spirit (Galatians 6:7-8).
C. When you're speaking the word, you're sowing seeds. The kingdom of God works in a process of seed time and harvest. It's a law and a principle. (1 Corinthians 3:6, Matthew 13:1, Genesis 8:22)

So, in this instance, we are learning what seed to sow in order to grow our spiritual ears. Here are more steps to understanding seed faith principles:

A. You must understand that, just as God is your source naturally and monetarily, God is also your source of spiritual development. (Acts 1:8)
B. Give and it shall be given back to you, pressed down shaken together (Luke 6:38). This is not only for money, but for whatever you need God to do in your life. God is a multiplier and when you sow time into the spirit, you are guaranteed a return. It doesn't matter if its time, money or devotion, time spent with God is time well spent and multiplied.

C. Expectation: Mark 11:24 reads, *"Therefore I say unto you, What things soever ye desire, when ye pray, believe that ye receive them, and ye shall have them."* This is an important principle to have because if we are going to ask God for an answer, he's going to answer us according to our faith. James 1:5-6 talks about how when a man needs wisdom, he should ask God, but he must ask in faith, not doubting. Wisdom is a gift from God. The same principles apply when we ask to interpret tongues or ask to receive tongues. I'm not saying that God is your genie, but if you're going to talk to him and spend time with him, you need to have faith that he will answer.

D. Asking, Believing, Speaking: If you never ask, you will never have what you need (James 4:2). You must also ask according to God's word. God is not going to give you the word of knowledge so that you can use it to make money. God won't give you the gift of prophecy to exploit people. You also must believe. You must have a conviction about what you asked God to do. If you ask God for a gift, or to flow in it, then you must believe that you have it when you ask. Most of us will ask God for an answer or an interpretation and then not even wait for an answer, but assume that God won't hear us. Lastly you must speak. What you speak is what you believe (2 Corinthians 4:13). If you believe that you hear from God and that God hears you, then you must speak it. If you truly believe that God has given you an interpretation, or a word of prophecy to release, then you must speak it.

Speaking and operating in your gift releases your faith. This is how you grow.

These are the steps that will help you grow, because remember, you're going to prophecy in PRORPORTION to your faith. Jesus said, *"If you have faith as a grain of mustard seed, you can say unto this mountain be removed and cast into the sea, and it shall obey"* (Matthew 17:20).

You must see your seed not as small, but as a process. Don't focus on the smallness of your faith but understand the process. You are now putting yourself in position to prophecy (speak) to the mountains in your life. Remember, there is no activation unless you speak what you believe. So, let's look at the steps.

Faith comes by hearing and hearing by the word. You must know what you have access to in order to be activated. Even as you read this book, confess the promises of God. Tell your mountains to move. The word says, *"I will pour out my spirit on all flesh, and your sons and daughters shall prophecy!"* (Acts 2:17)

Once you hear the promises, ask in faith not doubting. If you desire a gift, then ask for it! (1 Corinthians 14:1, James 1:5). You must ask with the correct motive and not doubt. If you have the desire, then its likely God placed it there.

Spend time sowing into the spirit of God. As you begin to spend time with God, he will trust you with more and you will learn to recognize God's thoughts. The more you sow, the more you grow. You don't have to let the world know that you're spending quality prayer time with God. The growth will be manifested.

This is a common mistake many Christians make. They spend time in prayer so that they can sound a trumpet to be seen. They operate in gifts to be seen rather than to build up the kingdom. The second you seek the glory of men, you lose the reward or the glory of God. (Matthew 6:5)

Make sure that you are faithful over what God has shared with you. As you grow, God will begin to show you the secrets of men's hearts. God wants to know He can trust you with secret things. If you're faithful over a little, God will make you ruler over much (Matthew 25:23). Now you are working the faith process. Like the Bible says, first the seed, then the blade, then the ear, then the corn in the ear. The final phase is reproduction. (Mark 4:26)

Remember, a tree or a plant cannot eat its own fruit (Galatians 5:22). The fruit of the tree is for reproduction. Now, some people can only operate at seed level. The word is in them, but it is seed. Some people operate in the blade level. The seed is growing but it's not mature enough to reproduce. The end game is not just to be someone that's anointed, but to impart the anointing.

Here are more tips to help on your journey:

A. Saving faith is different from faith that you use to prophecy. So, just because God doesn't give you some wild prophetic experience, it doesn't mean you don't know Him.
B. Spiritual senses like ears, eyes, and even smelling must be developed. More on that later.
C. Your ears can become dull of hearing, or even sleep. If you used to be a wonder prophet years ago, but haven't heard from God in a while, you may

need to find out what happened and repent.
(Hebrews 5:11-12)

D. God talks to you in various ways and God's voice
can come to you in visions or by other means.

E. Most of the time, God really talks to you. He
doesn't speak in an audible voice, he speaks in
thoughts. In fact, I wouldn't recommend at all that
you look for God to speak to you in voices. If you
look for voices, you will often find the wrong one.
God speaks to you mainly in thoughts and scripture
(John 14:26). The Holy Spirit's job is to bring the
word back to your remembrance. So, if you don't
hear voices, don't be ashamed and don't beat
yourself up. As you spend time with the Holy Spirit,
you will learn to recognize the thoughts of God.
Remember, words are spirits. Thoughts are spirits.
Jesus said, *"the words that I speak to you are spirit
and life"* (John 6:62).

F. Not every Christian has the same gifts and graces.
For one individual, they may see visons and
prophecy easier than others. For another, they may
have more wisdom. You must know your grace and
giftings.

I'd like to share one more thing before I close this
chapter. The scripture in Isaiah 55:8 says, *"For my ways
are not your ways, and my thoughts are not your thoughts,
says the Lord."* Most people will just stop there and fail to
read the rest of the scripture or understand what God is
saying. God's thoughts are indeed higher than ours. That's
why when he shares his thoughts with us, they are
intrusive.

Verse 10: *"For as the rain cometh down, and the snow from heaven, and returneth not thither, but watereth the earth, and maketh it bring forth and bud, that it may give seed to the sower, and bread to the eater:"*.
Remember, the earth is your heart! (Matthew 13:19). God made provision for the word to rain down on you! God made provision to give seed to the sower and bread to the eater. See God as he sees you! You are good ground! Seek him and know his thoughts!

There is a story in the Bible concerning Thomas. John 20:25 talks about how Thomas was not with the other disciples when Jesus showed up. Thomas made up in his mind that he would not believe until he felt the hole in Jesus' side and felt the nail prints in his hands. Thomas was looking for sense realm evidence to prove his faith rather than walking by faith. When we speak in tongues, we don't understand what we are saying. When we give the word of knowledge, we don't have prior knowledge that the information is true. If we did, then it would not be supernatural.

You must understand that when you operate in the gifts, you're operating by faith and not by sight. You are trusting by faith that what God has spoken to you is true. You are trusting by faith that your father hears you. You are believing that by faith, you have spent seed time building yourself up in your most holy faith. You are believing by faith that even though your tongues sound like babble to the natural ears, you are speaking mysteries. Don't be a doubting Thomas. Prophecy according to your faith!

The Power of the Prayer of Faith

Now, the scripture says this; *"Is any sick among you? Let him call for the elders of the church; and let them pray over him, anointing him with oil in the name of the Lord: And the prayer of faith shall save the sick, and the Lord shall raise him up; and if he have committed sins, they shall be forgiven him"* (James 5:14-15). Now, besides the fact that God saves you when He heals you (more on that later), there is an important principle that God wants to show you here. If you notice in scripture, anytime that there is activation, the prayer of faith comes first.

Notice that before God will heal, He wants the prayer of faith. Look at James 1:5. God instructs us that if we are going to ask for wisdom, we need the prayer of faith. In 1st Corinthians 14:13, when he instructs us to pray that we might interpret. Do you think that you should pray in faith or without faith? He says in the same chapter to ask for spiritual gifts and especially that we might prophecy. Do you think you should ask doubting? What about the word of knowledge? What about miracles? Do they operate without faith? The bottom line is that there can be no activation without faith, and God is waiting for a faith-filled prayer to move.

But what is the prayer of faith? To put it simply, a prayer of faith is a prayer audibly, that adheres to God's words, that is sincere, and that is made with the expectation that God will indeed answer. Let's find a biblical example to prove it. The scripture says In James 1:5, *"If any man lacks wisdom let me ask of God"*. So, the first part is asking for something that God has promised in his word. The wisdom he is asking for is something that God has promised us.

The second part is the asking part. The Bible talks about how we have not because we ask not. But you must stand in full assurance of faith. As we have said before, if your conscience is guilty and you don't believe God hears you, then it's hard to stand in confidence. Another thing that hinders us is unforgiveness. Now you can fool other people, but you can't fool the spirit of God. You must ask and be confident in full assurance of faith.

"Who gives liberally and without reproach." Again, this is a gift that God pours out liberally and freely. But we have not because we ask not. And we ask amiss so that we may look good! Remember, Eve saw a tree that was desired to make her wise? (Genesis 3:6). Wise to who? Do we want to just look good or edify the church?

"But let him ask in faith not wavering. For he who wavers is like a wave of the sea driven with the wind and tossed" (James 1:6). You see, you must be fully convinced that if you ask for it, God hears you. Prayer is a two-way conversation. You must be convinced that you hear from God and that God hears from you. If you desire to ask for the word of knowledge, then believe that he has given it to you. As you sit in quiet waiting for an answer, God will deal with you. But without faith, there is no activation.

"For let not that man think that he shall receive any thing of the Lord. A double minded man is unstable in all his ways" (James 1:7-8). Think of it this way: God wants to build you up in faith but you can't build something on an unstable sea. Remember, to every man is given a measure of faith. You're going to activate according to your faith. No faith? No power. Little faith? A little power. Most holy faith? All power.

Teaching Guide

What is the definition that we gave for Seed Faith
Principle?

What does Galatians 6:7 teach us about sowing?

What does Mark 4:6 tell us about spiritual growth?

Why is it important to grow your spiritual ears?

The Bible says faith comes by hearing and hearing by
what?

What is the final purpose of a tree's fruit?

3

Introduction to the Gifts of Utterance:

Speaking In Tongues

It was sometime around 2010 that I worked a job as a custodian. During this time, I would pray every night around 10:00 pm. During one of these nights as I was working, I prayed, and prayed, but didn't feel like God was answering or hearing me. I prayed in tongues and God began to scold me about something.

You see, I was praying but I wasn't present. My mind would wander off into other things. God began to give me a lesson at that moment in prayer. He told me to never pray on autopilot. He made me respect His presence by teaching me to prepare my mind before prayer. I learned a lot of valuable lessons about prayer and praying in tongues over the years I would like to share.

First off, what does it mean to speak in tongues and how is it relevant to today? The Greek word for tongues is 'Glossolalia', (from Greek *glōssa*, "tongue," and *lalia*, "talking"). This means that God gives you the ability to speak supernaturally in a language you don't understand.

This will also be your introduction to gifts of utterance. Utterance means that the gift must be spoken to operate (it would be difficult to speak in tongues by not actually speaking now, wouldn't it?).

You have gifts of utterance:

    A. Speaking in tongues
    B. Interpretation of tongues
    C. Prophecy

Then you have gifts of revelation:

    D. Discerning of spirits
    E. Word of wisdom
    F. Word of knowledge

You also have gifts of power:

    G. Gifts of healings
    H. The gift of faith
    I. The working of miracles

You also have callings that are offices. There are apostles, prophets, evangelists, pastors and teachers. I could write several books on these gifts alone, but this book will serve as an introduction to gifts of the spirit. There are other motivational gifts and operations, but we will mostly focus on these spiritual gifts for this section.

The gifts of utterance all must be spoken. Utterance is about your communication; communication with God, and God communicating with you individually or his people. While the revelation gifts deal with information, or the unveiling of something, the speaking gifts deal with the voice of God. The revelation gifts reveal the mind of God. The power gifts, as you guessed, show the power of God. Here is more on tongues.

How Do I Speak In Tongues?

For the record, I cannot teach a person to speak with tongues. It's a gift. But I can give you biblical principles to guide you. Acts 2:1 is a basic guide.

A. Just like on the day of Pentecost, you must seek the gift. You must desire it and wait for it.
B. You must ask for it. The Bible talks about in James 4:2 having not because you ask not.
C. You must believe that as you begin to speak, God is giving you the utterance.
D. At some point, God's spirit will come and sit on you or overshadow you.
E. When you hear the sound, you must speak it. When I say sound, I don't mean an audible noise, but in your thoughts.
F. When you believe as the scripture says, the tongues and the Holy Spirit will flow out of you and out of your belly. The ancient Hebrews saw the belly as the center of your being. When we say out of your belly, we are talking about from your inner most being or your spirit man. Sometimes you will feel an unction to speak or a pull to speak. You will know instantly that God wants your tongue to move.

The language can be an earthly language or the language of angels.

The Bible clearly states that unknown tongues are NOT meant to be understood by you, unless you or someone else has the gift of interpretation (1 Corinthians 14:2). So, if someone is speaking in a language that they are familiar with, this is not the gift.

Keep in mind that speaking in tongues can be an angelic language (1 Corinthians 13:1). So, it's not meant to be understood by you in any way shape or form. I say this because when you first start speaking, your tongues may not be pretty. Don't be discouraged. Don't let people convince you that your tongues are not real. The only tongues that are fake are tongues spoken not in faith. To clarify, you have the gift of tongues and then you have diverse tongues. More on diverse tongues later.

Speaking in tongues comes from your spirit.

When you speak in tongues, your spirit prays, but your understanding is unfruitful (1 Corinthians 14:14). This means that you are using your faith you speak. You open your mouth to pray but the spirit gives the mystery or the utterance (Acts 2:4).

Speaking in tongues is not required for salvation, but you should speak.

The Bible says that if you confess with your mouth and believe in your heart, you shall be saved (Romans 10:9). It even says that a prayer of faith will not only heal the sick, but his sins will be forgiven (James 5:15). Now, tongues are a sign that you believe but they are not a requirement. In fact, the Bible asks, do all speak with tongues? Do all interpret? (1 Corinthians 12:30). The answer is obviously no. There are even instances in scripture where people received the Holy Spirit and prophesied first before they ever spoke in tongues.

Speaking in tongues is a promise in the scripture.

Mark 16:17 clearly states that the gift of tongues is a sign of you being a believer.

Speaking in tongues builds you up in the spirit.

When you pray in tongues, you are building yourself up in your most holy faith. This is the kind of faith that brings you into God's presence. It's important to have this kind of devotion and time with God. When you do this, again, you're sowing into the spirit. This is how God trains your ear for the prophetic. When you see someone who really is anointed and can flow in God's presence, it's because they spent time in private talking with the Lord. There is a principle that the Father that sees in secret likes to reward you openly (Matthew 6:5-6). It's important to rule your heart and your spirit well because it's your responsibility to rule your spirit (1 Corinthians 14:32, Proverbs 16:32, Proverbs 25:28).

We will learn later that part of prophecy is to edify the church, but tongues are for edifying yourself. Not the flesh, but it's building up your spirit man in the things of God (1 Corinthians 14:4). When you pray in tongues, in the spirit, it is the equivalent of you prophesying to yourself. The God in you is speaking to you! Do you believe it? Let's look at Acts 2:17. The apostle talks here about God pouring out his spirit on all flesh. Why would we use this scripture for speaking in tongues? Because the tongues, when used this way, are prophetic! The same thing happens when you don't understand what you're saying. You speak mysteries in the spirit, only you're speaking to yourself.

I also want to remind you that when you pray in the Holy Ghost, He partners with you supercharging your prayers. God wants to quicken, or make alive, your mortal body (Romans 8:11). This is how you make your spirit man strong against sin. Remember, pray so you won't enter temptation. The spirit is willing, but the flesh is weak. (Matthew 26:41)

There are diverse tongues and prayer tongues.

Sometimes you will receive a tongue that's in a natural foreign language that you don't know. This is called diverse tongues. These are sometimes given on a mission field. A person who speaks the foreign language is often the recipient with amazing results. This type of tongue doesn't require a gift of interpretation. The hearer just knows the language naturally. (1 Corinthians 12:28, Acts 2:7-9)

For instance, there are testimonies of a person praying in tongues who doesn't speak Arabic, but the people nearby who know Arabic glorify God and are amazed at the person praying in a language they have never learned.

You can pray in tongues at-will.

Remember, you don't have to sit for hours and wait to see if God will give you a tongue. As we have discussed before, *"The spirit of the prophets is subject to the prophet"* (1 Corinthians 14:32). You can turn it on and turn it off. It's important to know and understand this. Many Christians fall into error because they think that God just takes you over like a robot and you have no control over yourself. But it's written in the Bible that God isn't the author of confusion. 1 Corinthians 14:28 says that if you don't have an interpreter, then you should keep silent. God wouldn't ask you to keep silent if you couldn't.

This is important. There are times to pray in a meeting with the understanding and there is a time to pray in tongues. If I am leading in prayer, then how will the people I'm leading know what I'm saying? So, there is a time to pray in the spirit and a time to pray with understanding. Therefore, if you're praying in a tongue and no one can interpret, it's better to pray to yourself or ask God for an interpretation (1 Corinthians 14:27).

You can ask God for interpretation.

In the next chapter, we are going to discover how this principle can and will be transformational for you. To put it simply, we have already read how God wants you to ask if no person can interpret.

In the next chapter, we will also explore how when you put these two gifts together, you get a lot of utility and spiritual growth from the gift of tongues. You can sing or receive songs from tongues, receive teaching through tongues, receive prophecy and the word of knowledge. Let's explore in the next chapter the gift of interpretation and get a full understanding of the utterance gifts.

So, just to recap:

a) The gift of tongues is an utterance gift.
b) You speak in tongues by faith.
c) There is a difference between unknown tongues and diverse tongues.
d) In the spirit you speak mysteries.

e) At times when you receive tongues, the Holy Ghost will overshadow you or sit on you.

f) When the Holy Spirit overshadows you, listen for tongues in an inner voice.

g) You don't need tongues for salvation, but you should speak in tongues.

h) Praying in tongues builds you up.

God wants you to use your tongues in devotion. When you pray like this, you're maximizing the gift of God in you. The things of God are in the spirit; go and get them. God wants you to develop a habit of praying in the spirit.

Teaching Guide

What is a gift of utterance?

What does the word Glossolalia mean?

Where does speaking in tongues come from?

List one scripture in the Bible that promises speaking in tongues.

Am I going to hell if I don't speak in tongues?

What are diverse tongues?

4

Interpretation of Tongues

It was way back in 1999. We would have an old-fashioned pentecostal-style church service which would evolve into worship. Suddenly, someone would stand up and speak in tongues in a booming voice almost like a trumpet. The room would grow very quiet at the sound. All music would stop. People listened intently. The ushers would monitor the room for children misbehaving. Suddenly, another person would stand up and begin to prophecy over the room, beginning in a loud booming voice saying, "THUS SAITH THE LORD!" This was my first experience with interpretation of tongues.

So, what is the gift of interpretation of tongues? To put it simply, the gift gives you the ability to supernaturally understand what's being said in tongues and bring forth an accurate understanding. The Greek word for interpretation is 'dierméneuó' (pronounced dee-er-main-yoo'-o). It means to explain thoroughly or by implication to translate. Keep in mind that you are speaking in tongues from your spirit. So, you may speak in tongues for less than a minute, but the interpretation may be longer. In the spirit, the tongue-talker is speaking mysteries (1 Corinthians 14:2).

Here are more facts about the gift of interpretation.

You can interpret your own tongues.

If you are in prayer or in a meeting and there are tongues, but no one there to interpret them, you can ask God to interpret. This isn't limited to just other people's tongues, but your own tongues as well. The Bible specifically says, *"Wherefore let him that speaketh in an unknown tongue pray that he may interpret"* (1 Corinthians 14:13). This is very specific. If you're praying in an unknown tongue with no interpreter, you only edify yourself. With an interpreter, you edify the body (1 Corinthians 14:1-13). Do you believe that if you have the gift that it only works when others speak in tongues?

You can interpret other people's tongues.

God wants you to ask Him for gifts (1 Corinthians 14:1-13). If you are in a meeting and there is someone coming forth with a tongue, you can ask God and He will give you an understanding. This opens powerful possibilities.

When you ask God for an answer, He is faithful to show up.

How do I know? I walked it out. I tried it. I received a challenge from an evangelist to pray in tongues for five minutes and then ask God for an answer or an interpretation. God showed up then and is always faithful to show up when I pray in faith.

Prophecy is not the only gift that comes with interpretation.

So, if you haven't noticed there is an entire chapter in the Bible devoted to spiritual gifts of utterance. If you read carefully in 1 Corinthians 14:6, you will find a nugget. Paul writes saying, *"Now brethren, if I come to you speaking with tongues, what shall I profit you, except I speak to you either by revelation, or by knowledge, or by prophesying or by doctrine.*" So, if you're speaking in tongues, how is it that you can get teaching or revelation if the words are not understood? The answer is the gift of interpretation.

Revelation and word of knowledge comes through interpretation. (1 Corinthians 14:6)

Sometimes, if you ask God for an interpretation instead of getting a prophetic message for the church, it will activate the word of wisdom word of knowledge, or discernment, in you. This is what the scripture means by revelation.

I had an instance at my job where I was in prayer earlier and asked God to interpret. The anointing was heavy on me and I noticed things as people walked by. Suddenly, a man walked past me and I heard the Holy Ghost say to me, "Reverend." I was nervous because it had been years since I really flowed in the word of knowledge, but I stepped out on faith. I called out to the man "Hey, Reverend." The man told me that he was a reverend in an old church and had gotten into trouble. I began to praise and magnify God for being so real in my life.

I want to point out how God has never failed to give me what to say in my teaching ministry after prayer in tongues. Wisdom comes on me to complete the task. Again, we are not talking about natural knowledge, but the gift of supernatural knowledge will come through interpretation.

Prophecy: this is the most common use for the gift of interpretation when you have tongues. Come together with interpretation, they are equal to prophecy. (1 Corinthians 14:5)

Teaching: I was inspired by the Holy Spirit to write this book through the gift of interpretation of tongues. In fact, with most of this book, God gave me exactly what to write in prayer and meditation. I want to encourage all teachers of the word that praying in the spirit will open a much higher dimension to your teaching. It's one thing to study, but there are times when I'm praying in the spirit and the words nearly leap off the page.

At times, I can start praying in tongues and the Holy Spirit will say, 'add this' or 'you forgot this'. There are teachings over the last 50+ years that have come to the body of Christ through interpretation, things like seed faith principle, all given to great teachers. I cannot emphasize enough how getting in the spirit will empower you.

Inspired Nugget

I was praying in the spirit very recently while driving and I heard the Holy Spirit say to me, "The tongue of the learned." I began to research this almost immediately and found this in Isaiah 50:4: *"The Lord has given me the tongue of the learned that I may speak a word in season to him that is weary."* I realized that there are tongues that are prophetic, and there are tongues that are specifically for teaching. I want to encourage teachers to not only continue to study, but to pray in the spirit for a timely word.

Another Bible translation says the tongue of wisdom. Then he says this in the same verse: *"He wakeneth my ear to hear as the learned."* Remember, just because you're a teacher, don't close yourself off to developing your spiritual ears. Allow God to awaken your ears in the spirit. Your teaching will become richer and timely.

Singing/Songs: Again, the scripture talks about singing in the spirit. Some people have written their best material and sung the most anointed songs after praying in the spirit.

What does interpretation of tongues feel like?

I had an experience recently in which I felt a strong impression to call someone. As soon as I started to speak to them on the phone, I heard with my inner voice, 'a tongue to speak in.' After I began to speak, I heard the spirit prompt me to interpret. When I finished speaking, the person encouraged me that the things that were spoken were correct and right on time.

This is one of the ways that God uses me. At times there might feel like a pulling or a compelling to speak in tongues. At other times, I hear the tongues in the spirit and then speak. If I speak for a while and nothing comes to me, I will pray to the Lord so that I can interpret. If nothing comes still, I listen for a while and move on. Also, like we mentioned before, the gift of interpretation can activate other gifts. So, pay attention to things around you.

The Radio Station. There is an amazing evangelist named Tom Scarillia that gave me insight into interpretation. Radio waves are all around us. They are constantly broadcasting. The Holy Spirit is the same way. He is constantly thinking of you. In fact, he said, *"I know the thoughts I have towards you says the Lord, thoughts of Good and not evil, to give you an expected end"* (Jeremiah 29:11). So, God is constantly thinking about you. He said, *"what is man that thou art MINDFUL of him or the son of man that thou visit him"* (Hebrews 2:6). So, God's mind is FULL of you. When a person is mindful of you, they are constantly concerned.

So, God:

    A. Is very mindful of you and,

    B. God likes to visit you.

Now back to my radio scenario. God is always broadcasting, but we are not always on the correct channel. God is mindful of us, but our radio antenna is switched off. If you will learn to tune in, you will find out that God always wants to talk and visit. Now, remember to keep a humble mind. The things we are learning here are spiritual principles, so they will work every time. I don't want you to become a devil just because you know how to get an answer or gift from the Lord, but let it be for the building of the body that you seek to excel.

Also, remember the spirits of the prophets are subject to the prophets. We are learning how to tune into God, but at times you will be surprised by what He says. There are times when I had heavy burdens on my mind and wanted to talk about things like money, cars and houses. I expected to get some grand revelation, or word of knowledge, and instead God gave me teaching. If you really desire this gift, let's pray for activation today as you read this book:

Father, in the name of Jesus, we praise and thank you for your word today. God, we thank you for exceedingly precious promises. God, we lay aside every weight and sin that easily besets us. We repent from every evil motive. God, we come before you today touching and agreeing. We come together agreeing for activation in the spirit. God, give us the gift of interpretation on today. You said you would pour out your spirit on all flesh and that we would see visions.

And God, we declare today that we will be activated. God, we declare that we will walk worthy of the gift and vocation in which we are called. We will use this gift for your glory and to edify the church. In Jesus' name, amen.

Teaching Guide

Explain the gift of interpretation of tongues.

What gifts or answers can come out through interpretation?

Is the gift of interpretation a power gift or revelation gift?

What does 1 Corinthians 14:13 say that you should do if you pray in a tongue with no one else to interpret?

How do you receive the gift of interpretation?

What is an utterance?

What chapter in the Bible talks almost exclusively about gifts of utterance?

5

The Gift of Prophecy

"And it shall come to pass in the last days, saith God, I will
pour out of my Spirit upon all flesh: and your sons and
your daughters shall prophesy, and your young men shall
see visions, and your old men shall dream dreams: And on
my servants and on my handmaidens I will pour out in
those days of my Spirit; and they shall prophesy:"
-Acts 2:17

So, we hear the word prophecy a lot in some church circles. These days, it seems like everyone wants to be a prophet or prophecy. But what is the gift of prophecy and what is its purpose? In this chapter we will delve into the primary gift of utterance and learn to understand it.

The word 'prophecy' comes from the Greek word 'prophéteuó' (pronounced prof-ate-yoo'-o). It means to foretell or to speak inspired speech. But the gift of prophecy has more than one use. The gift of prophecy is a speaking gift, so prophesying is about what God is saying. The word of knowledge and wisdom are about what God is revealing.

You can have the word of knowledge, wisdom, and discernment and see something, but what you see may not be what God wants to say in that hour. Prophesying is all about what God wants to say. This is why when you see or hear things spiritually, it's important to ask God if He wants the vision released. If someone has a secret sin, and you see it, you can seriously scar a person if you expose them publicly. We must be led by the spirit of God.

In 1 Corinthians 14:1, the Bible talks about desiring the best gifts, but especially prophecy. I have always wondered why God would choose this gift over the others as one of the best. And then, it occurred to me that prophecy is one of the gifts (along with interpretation) that allows for other gifts to flow with it. Words of knowledge, wisdom, and discernment will often come along with prophecy. Healing can be delivered through prophecy. Instructions for miracles will come through prophecy. Prophecy is like a big three lane highway that other gifts can flow through.

There is disagreement, and in some cases confusion, about the different gifts in the church. A good prophetic word will often have elements of the word of wisdom and the word of knowledge in it. Just take the book of Revelations for instance. The entire book is a prophecy, but not everything in the book foretells something. Many elements in the book contain insights and words of wisdom.

Inspired Nugget

I want to take a moment to interrupt your train of thought and help you to understand that. Here, we are going to start calling your spiritual senses gates. There is an eye gate, both natural and spiritual. There is an ear gate, and so on. When the Bible says to guard your heart, he literately means to stand guard over what comes in and what goes out (Proverbs 4:23).

So, when I say ear gate, I am talking about your faculty for spiritual hearing. And when I'm talking about your eye gate, I am discussing your faculty for spiritual perception. Now, it's your responsibility to guard the gates or doors to your heart and your spirit man. Remember, words are spirits. Thoughts are spirits. Do you let natural perception cloud or cancel your faith? Job said it perfectly when he wrote, *"I made a covenant with mine eyes"* (Job 31:1).

How do I guard the gates of my heart? When I worked as a prison guard, it was my job to stand at the door and control movement. It was my job to stand in a tower, sometimes armed, and confront intruders. No one got in and nothing got out without being properly challenged. It's the same in the spirit. Do you just accept any thought and spirit that comes to you? Do you challenge anger and hurt? I used to ask the inmates, "Where are you going? Where did you come from? Identify yourself!" I guarded the doors. When thoughts come to you, you should recognize quickly if it's a thought from God or if it's an angry thought.

When emotions come to you, we should have the emotional intelligence and maturity to question emotions. Remember, strong meat belongs to those who by reason of use have their senses exercised to discern good and evil (Hebrews 5:14). It is the same way with the gifts. Everything that is seen isn't meant to be pronounced in the streets and highlighted. Even Daniel discussed some things in the spirit being sealed. (Daniel 12:4)

Prophetic Responsibility. Another part of guarding the gates or keeping your heart is watching what goes out. The mouth is the only gate where you must watch what goes in and what is coming out. You must understand that when you give a prophecy or word of knowledge, it opens people's hearts to influence.

In 1 Corinthians 14, it talks about the secrets of men's hearts being revealed. If God is going to give you this gift, then you must be responsible when you open people up. There have been constant instances in my life where a person will give a warning about something or give a dire prophecy, but they don't have the wisdom to show a person how to manage it. <u>A problem with no solution can bring despair.</u> Some people prophecy out of season. Again, just because you see something, doesn't mean that you must rush to release it. Be slow to speak, swift to hear, and slow to wrath.

Another common mistake is using your prophetic gift out of anger or frustration. Just because we are angry doesn't mean God is angry. We must know voices. There are many voices in the world that we must discern and familiarize ourselves with. There is a voice for our culture, a voice from our flesh, demonic voices, and even the voice from our soul and our desire. The only voice that we want to speak from is the voice of God. As we grow, we will learn not to entertain other voices. This is again why we must guard our heart and emotions. If we allow anger, lust and prejudice to speak to us, how can we hear God clearly? It's our responsibility to guard our hearts!

There are several other definitions in Hebrew. Let's examine a few.

Nabi. The word Nabi in Hebrew means to bubble up, to proclaim the words of God. So, some people, when they operate in the gift of prophecy, they operate mainly from there ear and mouth gate. Jeremiah 20:9 said it perfectly when he said it's like fire, shut up in his bones.

Roeh. It means to see or perceive. Or a better translation is what the Bible calls a seer. A seer is someone who God speaks through primarily through the eye gate. Some people have an eye gate focus and some people have an ear gate focus. People with a seer focus tend to operate in the revelation gifts a lot more.

Hozeh is one who sees or perceives. This is primarily in relation to music, but it's also used for a person that counsels kings. The council can be natural or Hozeh prophetic (1 Kings 17:13).

Let's recap. There are:

A. Nabi prophets, who the prophecy just bubbles up out of.
B. Seer prophets, who see and perceive things. They operate a lot in dreams and visions.
C. Prophetic counselors, who have the gift of wisdom along with the gift of prophecy.
D. Prophetic musicians, who God will use to worship and prophecy through song.

Now, if you can recall, Paul writes an entire chapter specifically dealing with the gifts of utterance. In this chapter, he explains thoroughly the rules for prophecy. The Bible says in 1 Corinthians 14:3, *"He that prophesieth speaks unto men edification, exhortation, and comfort."* So, as we can see here, prophecy is not just for predicting the future. There is also another scripture that says, *"Neglect not the gift that is in you, that was given to you by prophecy, and the laying on of hands by the elders"* (1 Timothy 4:14). So, we see here another use for prophecy.

So far, we know that prophecy is for:

A. Edification
B. Exhortation
C. Comfort
D. Impartation
E. Direction/Forthtelling
F. Worship

Edification. The number one reason for prophecy in the church is for edification; to build up the body of Christ and to mature the people. Someone speaking through the spirit of God will never seek to tear apart God's church. There might be correction, but it will always edify. There may be conviction. With the conviction, a way out or repentance will be presented. True prophecy never condemns a church. Condemnation is when you see your wrongs, but there is no way out. True prophecy builds up and restores. Also, prophecy is designed to edify the body of Christ, not oneself. Any prophecy that glorifies the man rather than glorifies God is not a prophecy from God. Some people get just a few prophecies and get haughty and high-minded over the pastor or their leaders. Remember the chapter on prophetic integrity.

Moses is a good example of how to handle prophecy and leadership. In Numbers 12:1, it talks about how Aaron and Miriam allowed their bias, or racism, against the wife of Moses to cloud their judgment. The scripture says that they made this statement: *"And they said hath the Lord indeed spoken only to Moses? Hath he not spoken only by us?" And the Lord heard it."* Now, I don't have to complete the story for you to know that God was not pleased at all with this statement, even putting a curse on Miriam in the process. I'm here to let you know that leadership is a gift that should be respected just as much as prophecy.

Anyone that prophesies with this attitude is asking for trouble with God. Remember, prophecy builds up the body; it doesn't tear it down. Many people are running around with prophetic gifts who have broken away from a pastor or tried to tear down what God has built. They wonder why their lives are in shambles. Even if you're going to leave a church or have a problem with a leader, there is a right and wrong way to resolve issues (1 Timothy 5:19). True prophecy edifies or builds up the body.

Exhortation. Another job for prophecy is to exhort. When you exhort someone, you're encouraging or trying to bring the best out of them. True prophecy will always try and move you to be the best you. Even if the prophecy calls you to repent, or gives you a business idea, the spirit through prophecy encourages. There is no such thing as a depressing prophecy, which is another spirit. The spirit of God desires that you have life and have it more abundantly. Some people think that the gift of prophecy is for gossip, but true prophecy exhorts.

Comfort. It is no coincidence that the Holy Ghost is called the comforter (John 14:16, 26). True prophecy comforts the hurt and brokenhearted. Prophecy doesn't open wounds or throw salt in them. True prophecy doesn't confuse or annoy, it comforts. The scripture above also mentions how The Holy Spirit's job is to bring things back to your remembrance. That's his job as a comforter.

True prophecy will always line up with God's word. This is why a healthy understanding of the word is required to grow in the gift. If you don't know the word, or what God will or won't say, you leave yourself open to embarrassing mistakes. I had a woman ask me once upon a time, "If God showed you exactly what slot machine to play, would you play it?" She was angry because I answered no. I questioned why God would use the gift of prophecy in this manner for monetary gain or to gamble?!?! The true job of prophecy builds us up. It doesn't send us on worldly goose chases or to gamble.

Impartation. Prophecy is used in many cases to impart a gift into another believer. Remember, faith comes by hearing, and hearing by the word of God. This principle is not just for the written word but also for the spoken word. Therefore, it's of tantamount importance when prophesying to have leadership over you. When you're speaking into people's lives, even a simple mistake can cause a person to take a long detour in their life. A person may think they are called to pastor for years, when they are only called to the office of a prophet, simply because someone got it wrong. This is why you need oversight if you are prophesying a life event over someone's life. You telling a person to move away or become a pastor, or breakup with a person can have dire consequences.

You will see prophecy used many times in the development of others. The gift of prophecy should impart destiny and purpose. It should impart calling. Where there is no open vision in a church, there is no sense of calling or destiny imparted. Paul brought up with Timothy how his gifts were imparted through prophecy and the laying on of hands. We need this in our church.

Direction/Forth-Telling. This is one of the ways prophecy is used, but it's just one of many. The Bible talks about a man named Agabus the prophet in Acts 21:10: *"And as we tarried there many days, there came a down from Judea a certain prophet named Agabus. And when he was come unto us, he took Paul's girdle and bound his own hands and feet and said, thus saith the holy Ghost, so shall the Jews at Jerusalem bind the man that owneth this girdle, and deliver him unto the Gentiles."*

And here is another: Acts 11:28 reads, *"And there stood up one of them named Agabus and signifies by the spirit that there would be a great dearth throughout all of the world: which came to pass in the days of Claudius Caesar."*

Brothers and sisters, we need prophetic eyes in our church on today. If we would allow the prophetic gifts to flourish, we would not be caught so unaware. Things like covid would surely come, but they would not sneak up on us. A large part of the gift of prophecy is the guidance of prophecy.

Worship. Worship and the prophetic are closely related. All you need to do is read the book of Psalms to understand this. There is something about worship that invokes the prophetic and there is something about the prophetic that brings us into true worship. There is a certain level of worship that will automatically bring you into a prophetic realm.

But isn't the word of knowledge the same thing?

This is a common problem: telling the gift of prophecy, the word of knowledge, and discernment apart.

71

One of the reasons for is that the gift of prophecy usually brings other gifts with it. But here are tips to help you distinguish between them.

A. Prophecy is primarily for the church as a body. The word of knowledge, and discernment are for the individual. (1 Corinthians 14:4)
B. The word of knowledge and discernment deal with facts and perception. Prophecy delivers a message.
C. You don't have to speak discernment. In fact, most things you discover, you will hold silently.

If I prophecy, does this mean I'm a prophet?

The answer, in the strictest sense, is no! The Bible says in Acts 2:17 that God would pour his spirit out on all flesh. So, anyone can prophecy. If you ask for it, God will give it to you. But being a prophet is an entire other animal. Prophesying is a gift. Being a prophet is an office and a call. Anyone can prophecy, but not many are called to the office of a prophet.

I want you to be wary here. The ministry of a prophet looks glamorous, but it is a difficult walk. Many true prophets regret the spiritual warfare and difficulty surrounding the trials of a prophet. You may be motivated prophetically. You may even prophecy on a regular basis, but seek God when it comes to the call and the office. The old people used to say that 'there are some that were sent, and some that just went'.

How do I receive the gift of prophecy?

"Ask, and it shall be given you; seek, and ye shall find; knock, and it shall be opened unto you:" (Matthew 7:7). If you ask God and seek him for it, He will give it to

you. And the more you spend time with him in prayer talking to him, the more the gift will grow. God wants you to get in prayer and learn about him yourself. Like when mentioned before, in prayer you will grow. *"And the father who sees in secret will reward you openly"* (Matthew 6:6).

Let's pray:

Father, in the name of Jesus, we praise and thank you for your word today. God, we thank you for exceedingly precious promises. God, we lay aside every weight and sin that easily besets us. We repent from every evil motive. God, we come before you today touching and agreeing. We come together agreeing for activation in the spirit. God, give us the gift of prophecy on today. You said you would pour out your spirit on all flesh, and that your sons and daughters would prophecy. You said that we would see visions and dream dreams. God, we declare today that we will be activated. God, we declare that we will walk worthy of the gift and vocation in which we are called. GOD WE WILL USE THIS GIFT OF PROPHECY FOR YOUR GLORY AND TO EDIFY YOUR PEOPLE. In Jesus' name we pray, Amen.

Interview with Pastor Reagan

I want to present to you an interview with Pastor Latina Reagan, who is the head pastor of Cornerstone Family and Worship Church in Las Vegas Nevada. Pastor Tina has been in my life for nearly 30 years now and is one of the most prophetic people that I know. Here is a recent interview with her that will shed light on the gift of prophecy.

Minister Moreland: Hello Pastor Tina. Can you tell the readers a little bit about yourself and what you do?

Pastor Latina Reagan: I'm Pastor Tina. I pastor a church called Cornerstone Family and Worship Church here in Las Vegas, Nevada. Basically, that's what I do ministry-wise: pastoring within itself, and all that it encompasses. I'm a mom of three, I've been married 21 years, and that's basically it.

Minister Moreland: Pastor, in this book, I'm explaining aspects of the gift of prophecy. I explain how the anointing falls on people differently. I even describe how some people are Nabi prophets, which means the Holy Ghost operates in them like a bubbling up, or he uses primarily their ear gate to speak to them. And others, they operate more like a seer where he uses their eyes gates. How does God use you?

Pastor Latina Reagan: It's both.

Minister Moreland: What is the link in your opinion to obedience and operation? And I don't mean just obeying God, but your leaders in a set place?

Pastor Latina Reagan: Well, when it comes to the spirit of prophecy, growing up being around my dad and my brother, and understanding them being the pastor and apostle of the house, there is a submission that I have to God's order. And with submitting to God's order, I understand that just because God gives me something, doesn't mean it's an appropriate time to say it, and when to give it, and get a release from them, especially if it's over the house and is impacting the body. So, you never want to do anything without a level of covering. You never want to do anything as it relates to that leadership without them knowing it, especially if it's impacting the house.

The interaction with my leaders, mainly with what God showed me, was something mainly for the house. Or it was something for the house and how we are supposed to impact the community. That's where my function of prophetic gift flows. Every now and then, God will give me something more along the lines of what's happening in the nation, or what's going on in the nation and what steps we need to make. Now, that interprets into my pastor role messages that need to be given out.

Minister Moreland: How important is integrity when flowing in your gift?

Pastor Latina Reagan: You definitely have to have integrity, because if not, instead of using your gift to glorify God, you will start functioning out of talent and functioning in your gift independent of the spirit of God. At that point it's now flesh being glorified, and you're mixing spirit with flesh. Carnal results here are inevitable. So, you have to make sure that you have the spirit of God and integrity and making sure that your integrity is linked through the Holy Spirit. You don't want to do anything independent of the Holy Spirit.

Minister Moreland: If you are training a prophet or anyone gifted to walk in the anointing and office that God has called them to, what's the first and most important thing that you want them to know?

Pastor Latina Reagan: The foundations! Because even though you can operate in your gift, you need to be solid in foundation. Foundations meaning the word of God, the reason for the gift, how the gift operates, and how it moves.

As we taught in class, you have the pros and cons of one that's immature versus one that's mature. So, I would make sure that they understand those pros and those cons and then I would help them develop so that they don't fall into pitfalls. The prophetic gift is one that a lot of people seek after, and they try to target it because of the influence that's there. And if you're operating in that gift without or independent of the anointing of God, it can definitely be dangerous.

Minister Moreland: So, they want it because it's flashy, but they don't understand the integrity behind it, the rules behind it?

Pastor Latina Reagan: Right, and understanding where the source of everything comes from.

Minister Moreland: And not only that, but God is also dealing with me on the difference between the discerning of spirits and discerning from intuition. Because you can build natural discernment, but it's not the discerning of spirits.

Pastor Latina Reagan: You watch people's behavior and that's actually what the world does. If you look at what they call in the tech world *algorithms*, it's just the study of behavior. So, certain things people can predict simply because of the study of people and their behavior. If you have these traits, then you're apt to do these types of things. But yes, you need to see beyond the natural realm and into the spirit realm, and see what spirit you're dealing with and the roots of the spirit, not just dealing with the leaves and the branches.

This is why you need to be skillful in that because you can attack a leaf and the branch is still there. Some prophets or people that are not gifted or matured in that area can tear down and not build up. A skilled prophet knows how to tear down, and yet build up. People leave folks open and it causes more damage than good. There are so many different things and different components that are connected to that.

Minister Moreland: There is one more thing I want to share that God just gave me (laughs out loud). This is why I love talking to you, because we just flow off each other. How important is it as you walk in the gift of discerning of spirits to grow in love? My 1st inspiration for this book came from the scripture, "ye who are spiritual". It's from Galatians 6:1, and the Bible talks about how ye who are spiritual should restore. So many people in church feel like they are discerning something, but they are just beating up people.

Pastor Latina Reagan: The thing is this; the Bible says God is love. So, love is not just a fruit, but we have to understand who God is. And when you filter everything through that, and through the love of God, that will help make sure that you're not discerning out of your flesh, or some other hidden agenda. Again, you'll have the ability to see that God is showing you what to do, and that way he'll protect you from harming other people.

What people have to understand is there is accountability that you have in treating God's people right. As anointed and as gifted as God made Moses, when Moses hit that rock and called the folks out of their name, he had to suffer for that. So, love is crucial because even God said he chastises those whom he loves. There is a place in love even where he chastises us. We want to be sure of that love and that everything we do is rooted and grounded in him.

Minister Moreland: Thank you, pastor.

Pastor Latina Reagan: My pleasure.

Teachable Guide

Explain the gift of prophecy.

What scriptures in the Bible promise that prophecy is for us?

Is the gift of prophecy a power gift or revelation gift?

What does 1 Corinthians 14:3 tell about prophecy?

How do you receive the gift of prophecy?

What is the difference between an utterance gift and revelation gift?

What chapter in the Bible talks almost exclusively about gifts of utterance?

Why does the Bible say that prophecy is superior to only tongues?

If I prophecy does that make me a prophet?

Can anyone ask for the gift prophecy?

6

Introduction to the Gifts of Revelation:

The Word of Knowledge

It was way back in 1997. I lived in Grenada Hills, California with my mother at this time. I had just gotten saved and filled with the Holy Spirit. I was constantly on my face in prayer, seeking God's face and spending time with the Holy Spirit. At times I would lay there for what seemed like hours. One day, after watching a televised church service, the anointing fell heavily on me. I left the room and bumped into one of my mother's friends. Suddenly, I could see pictures or images in her face. I began to question her about a woman with freckles. I began to discuss with her things happening at her job. This was one of my first experiences with the word of knowledge.

So, as we talked about in other chapters, you have natural senses and you have spiritual senses. You have a natural perception and you have a spiritual perception. Prophecy uses the mouth of God. Discernment uses the five senses that God gave you. The word of knowledge uses the mind of God. In order to really flow in the word of knowledge, you must get to know and understand the thoughts and mind of God. Actually, all of the revelation gifts deal with the mind of God in one capacity or another.

Isaiah 55:7 talks about this: *"Let the wicked forsake his way, and the unrighteous man his thoughts: and let him return unto the LORD, and he will have mercy upon him; and to our God, for he will abundantly pardon."*

So, one of the first steps of allowing the mind of God to flow through you is getting rid of or forsaking evil thoughts. Here are some things to help you understand when the word of knowledge is in activation.

The gift is not simply called knowledge, but the word of knowledge. As we noted before, Jesus is the word made flesh. Now, you are flesh being made into the word. You must understand that the word of God is alive; it's living. The gifts are an outward manifestation of the living word. So, you have several things at work here:

A. It's the word of knowledge because you're speaking an inspired word.
B. It's the word of knowledge because it's a living breathing biblical principle and gift coming to life in you.
C. The word part is the living word.
D. The knowledge portion is God's thoughts. It's literally God sharing a portion of his omnipotence with you, letting you see what God is thinking about.

- The word of knowledge deals in facts and information. So, things like names, numbers, and true facts come to mind.
- The word of knowledge will come primarily through the eye and ear gates.
- The word of knowledge deals with the individual. Prophecy deals with the church body. If a person is singling you out, it's usually the word of knowledge.

- At times, you will see images or get single word phrases. Like I mentioned before, names, dates, times, facts.
- With discernment, you can feel things. Angels, demons, and even illnesses will be revealed. The word of knowledge again deals in facts.
- At times, you won't fully understand what you're seeing, so it helps to ask questions.
- The Holy Spirit will outline people at times.
- Remember, the word of knowledge can come through interpretation or be part of a bigger prophecy.

Asking questions can be very important when it comes to the word of knowledge. Like I mentioned before, I saw the image of what was going on in the woman's face. It was important for me to find out what it was that God wanted to do. With the word of knowledge, you may not completely understand everything you see.

Here are a few warnings about the word of knowledge:

A. It's no coincidence that the Bible talks about how knowledge puffs up, but love edifies. Never allow the gift to make you arrogant. This gift can be very flashy and very impressive, so it is frequently abused.

B. To a person with no discernment or spiritual understanding, the word of knowledge looks very similar to divination or soothsaying. Remember, the Holy Spirit's job is to point to Jesus. The thoughts of God will always point to Jesus and edify the body. The word of knowledge is God sharing his thoughts with you. God will never tell you to lie, steal, murder, or take advantage of people (1 John 4:1, John 14:26).

C. Use patience with the word of knowledge. If you see an image or a thought is impressed on you, don't rush and put your own understanding into the mix. But if you patiently ask God or the individual, God will reveal the answer or take you down the train of thought that he desires.

How do I operate in the word of knowledge?

Again, ask and it shall be given. It's very likely that if you have a desire to ask, God has put the desire in you. It takes asking and spending time in prayer to really flow in this gift. You don't want to be one of the kinds of people who hits and misses frequently. If you're reading this and asking, it's likely that God has cultivated the desire. I want you to say this prayer with me (shown further down), not just for this gift, but for every gift.

There is a process to nearly everything that God gives you. It normally goes in this order: revelation, understanding, and resolve or conclusion.

1. Revelation: What did you see or hear? Are you certain you heard it? Did it line up with God's word?
2. Understanding: Do you understand what you see? In the case of interpretation, the interpreter brings forth an understanding of what was heard in tongues. This is frequently an issue with dreams. A dream or prophecy that no one understands cannot edify. We operate always to bring clarity and understanding, not to be deep and unreachable. Being deep and hard to

understand only builds up the ego and not the body of Christ.

3. Resolve or Conclusion: What is the conclusion of what you saw? Does God want you to release it? What does God want you to convey or explain? You must be timely. If you move slowly, the time may pass and God will use someone else, or the matter might pass. If you move too fast, it may not be the time and the season. It's not only a matter of if God said it, but should you release it. Remember, God won't give you a new task if you're in disobedience from the last task. Remember Hebrews 5:14. Your spirit man is like a muscle. If you don't use it, it will become weak.

Father, in the name of Jesus, we praise and thank you for your word today. God, we thank you for exceedingly precious promises. God, we lay aside every weight and sin that easily besets us. We repent from every evil motive. God, we come before you today touching and agreeing. We come together agreeing for activation in the spirit. God give us the word of knowledge on today. You said you would pour out your spirit on all flesh, and that we would see visions. And God we declare today that we will be activated. God, we declare that we will walk worthy of the gift and vocation in which we are called. GOD WE WILL USE THIS GIFT OF WORD OF KNOWLEDGE FOR YOUR GLORY AND TO EDIFY YOUR PEOPLE. In Jesus name we pray, amen.

Can you show me a biblical example of the word of knowledge?

One of the best biblical examples of the word of knowledge is in John the 4:6-19. The Bible says this: "*Now Jacob's well was there. Jesus, therefore, being wearied with his journey, sat thus on the well: and it was about the sixth hour. There cometh a woman of Samaria to draw water: Jesus saith unto her, give me to drink. (For his disciples were gone away unto the city to buy meat.) Then saith the woman of Samaria unto him, how is it that thou, being a Jew, askest drink of me, which am a woman of Samaria? For the Jews have no dealings with the Samaritans. Jesus answered and said unto her, if thou knewest the gift of God, and who it is that saith to thee, give me to drink; thou wouldest have asked of him, and he would have given thee living water. The woman saith unto him, Sir, thou hast nothing to draw with, and the well is deep: from whence then hast thou that living water? Art thou greater than our father Jacob, which gave us the well, and drank thereof himself, and his children, and his cattle? Jesus answered and said unto her, whosoever drinketh of this water shall thirst again: But whosoever drinketh of the water that I shall give him shall never thirst; but the water that I shall give him shall be in him a well of water springing up into everlasting life. The woman saith unto him, Sir, give me this water, that I thirst not, neither come hither to draw. Jesus saith unto her, Go, call thy husband, and come hither. The woman answered and said, I have no husband. Jesus said unto her, thou hast well said, I have no husband: For thou hast had five husbands; and he whom thou now hast is not thy husband: in that sadist thou truly. The woman saith unto him, Sir, I perceive that thou art a prophet.* " The effect of the word of knowledge was very powerful and immediate!

Now, notice the things that Jesus did:

A. He was led directly to this woman by the word of knowledge, even sending his disciples away. The word of knowledge (or discernment) will at times point people out to you.
B. He deliberately led her in a spiritual conversation. The word of knowledge will lead you in either asking questions or move you into a spiritual conversation deliberately so that you may minister.
C. The word of knowledge will reveal the secrets of the heart. In this case, Jesus revealed facts about her that would be impossible to know.
D. The word of knowledge had such a powerful and dramatic effect on her that she immediately recognized that he was a man of God.
E. This is the reason the word of knowledge is mixed up a lot with prophecy.

Any other examples of the word of knowledge?

2 Kings 5:1-17 tells a great story that involves the word of knowledge. If you are not familiar with the story, there was a man named Naaman the leper that heard about a prophet in Israel. Naaman was finally healed after following the prophet's God-given instructions. Elisha refused to take anything from the man, but he had a servant who was greedy and prejudice. After Naaman left, the servant went secretly and lied to Naaman, so that he could receive money and clothing. Verse 26 says this:

"Did not my heart go with you when the man turned back from his chariot to meet you?"

Very gifted prophets can receive words of knowledge so strong that they will go to the place and see it. It's not an out of body experience, it's a God experience. Paul talks about how a man went to the third heaven and he didn't know if he was in his body or not (2 Corinthians 12:1).

How do I sharpen the word of knowledge?

Remember, usually when God speaks to you, his thoughts are disruptive. You might be thinking about what you will put on for dinner and suddenly a random thought will interrupt your thinking. You might be thinking about your favorite ice cream and suddenly you will see an image in your head. One of the main issues with the word of knowledge is that you can be exposed easily with it. For instance, with the gift of prophecy, God is talking about a future event. With the gift of wisdom or discernment, at times it can be hard to prove things as accurate. The word of knowledge deals in absolute facts. If I, for instance, tell you that you live at 264 Pine Street in Long Beach, California, the individual needs only to produce a driver's license showing a current address. If I tell you through prophecy that you will live on Pine Street, you must wait to prove it.

Again, the word of knowledge deals in facts. Therefore, with this gift you will be exposed easily if you can't hear God clearly. If you're going to operate in the gift, your prayer life and consecration must be solid. In reality, all of the gifts you must stay consecrated, but the word of knowledge puts you out there. When the Bible says these kinds only come out by fasting and praying, he's not just talking about casting out demons. He wants all demonstration to be empowered by a life of consecration.

Many preachers and ministers make the mistake of taking their gifts for granted. God poured into them like a man drinking from a fire hose when they first received his spirit. But now they have allowed spiritual eyes and ears to become dull. Remember this example and I'll repeat it over and over. You have natural eyes and spiritual eyes. You have natural senses and you have spiritual senses. You have a natural mind and a spiritual mind (the mind of Christ). If you don't use your natural muscles, they will atrophy. If you don't use your natural mind, it's called being sleep, or occupied. You can't use your spiritual senses or allow the mind of Christ to be in you if you haven't spent time in God's presence.

Notes on developing and exercising in the word of knowledge.

Now, for me being a teacher, I have had different experiences dealing with the word of knowledge. My experiences at the time of this writing haven't progressed to open visions or body experiences, but I have noticed that as you grow and operate in these gifts, there are levels. I truly believe God is speaking to us a lot more than we think but we allow our ears to become dull. We think God's thoughts are our thoughts and vice versa, but here is more to help you on this gift.

For the record, feeling infirmity and sickness in a part of your body is not the word of knowledge; that gift is discernment. We will deal with that in another chapter. Now keep in mind, if you're called to be a prophet, you will progress farther in some gifts naturally compared to a pastor or teacher for instance. We are learning how to be sensitive to God's spirit. The word of knowledge progresses by:

1. Thoughts come first. When God is speaking, the thoughts are normally disruptive to my thought process. For example, If I'm thinking of ice cream and the word of knowledge is operating, I may have a random thought that's relevant to ministry. Keep in mind, if I haven't said it before, the word of knowledge is almost always for an individual. When you're first starting, at times you will get bits of things that add up.

2. The second level is not just thoughts but impressions. Someone might say, 'I feel like God wants this.' There will be an urge or an unction to speak.

3. Third, you will have visions that start out as faint thoughts but grow as the gift develops. Sometimes the vision will flash in front of your face and will be unmistakable. I have had the experience of having a dream that was a word of knowledge. The dream was locked away or forgotten until I was near the individual at the proper time. Once you start seeing pictures like this, the gift is really flowing. If you have a thought in your mind that says, "red house", you could miss it easily. But when I tell someone, "I see you standing in front of a red house", and they just bought a house, the impact is stronger. Also, at this point God will start outlining people for you. He might make a person stand out from the crowd somehow.

4. Lastly, there is open vision with the word of knowledge. At this level you will have visions strong enough to make you believe you have left your body. You will literally go places and have details of things.

Can a person be wicked and use this gift?

The short answer is yes. A person can behave like a devil and still operate in gifts. The reason is that God doesn't give something and look to take it back. God doesn't give gifts and then take them away. Will the person receive all that God has to offer? No. Therefore, you can't just follow gifts of the spirit; you must have God's fruits (Galatians 5:22). Remember, Jesus said a good tree can't bring forth bad fruit. So, the one thing the devil cannot imitate is fruit. Unfortunately, the word of knowledge is one of the gifts that the devil imitates the most.

Inspired Nugget

There is a portion of scripture in 1 John 2:20 that says, *"But you have an anointing from the holy one and you know all things"*. As I began to meditate on this scripture, God gave me a quote. The anointing here is the charisma. It's the supernatural ability to do or know something. So, the first thing that we establish is that the ability and this knowledge comes supernaturally from God, and like the scriptures says is true.

You don't know everything, but all things can be known. When you receive the word of knowledge, nearly everything is on the table and can be known. But you don't know everything at once; you know in parts. Your God is independent. If you knew everything within yourself, then you would not need the supernatural. But the word of knowledge will reveal things to you by the spirit of the living God.

Teachable Guide

Explain the gift of word of knowledge.

What scriptures in the Bible promise that word of knowledge is for us?

Is the word of knowledge a power gift or revelation gift?

Read John 4:1-29. Show me an example of the word of knowledge.

How do you receive the word of knowledge?

What is the difference between an utterance gift and revelation gift?

What chapter in the Bible talks almost exclusively about gifts of utterance?

Where does the Bible talk about word knowledge?

If I operate in the word of knowledge, does that make me a prophet?

Can anyone ask for the word of knowledge?

7

The Discerning of Spirits

(1 Corinthians 12:10, Hebrews 4:12)

Sometime in early April 2019, I was online dating on a Christian website. Suddenly, a woman popped up on my screen. She was one of the most beautiful women that I had seen. As soon as I looked at her picture, I felt an irritation in my spirit. The Holy Spirit began to talk to me immediately and tell me that I would not be able to call this person. Being a fool, I decided to call anyway. I called no less than three times, but I got nothing but static. The person on the other end texted me an excuse that the phone wasn't working and that we should just text. God was trying to warn me that the person was false, or what we call online, a catfish. I had no idea until that point that you could discern things from a photo.

I have many other stories, but in this chapter we will dive into the discerning of spirits. Over the last few years, God has put me through different scenarios and allowed me to experience a higher level of discernment. But what is discernment and how do we define it?

A. The gift of discernment allows you to see and be aware of things in the spirit realm.
B. To discern means to judge or make a judgement. This is why this gift is so crucial in the body.

I want to take you to a verse that explains discernment in detail. Hebrews 5:14 reads, *"But strong meat belongs to them who by reason of use have their senses exercised to discern good from evil"*. So here is what we establish:

    A. You have natural senses, and you have spiritual senses.
    B. Your spiritual senses only grow by using them, just like a muscle.
    C. The more you exercise these senses, the more your discernment will grow.
    D. Your spiritual senses are touch, taste, smell, hearing, and sight.
    E. Just like you use your natural senses to be aware of your surroundings, God wants to awaken your eyes and ears unto the things of the spirit.

Notice how in Hebrews 5:11, he calls them dull of hearing. God wants to develop your inner man/woman! Also keep in mind that we read before how when you ask for interpretation, it can activate other gifts (1 Corinthians 14:6). When the Bible talks about revelation, discernment is one of the revelation gifts. Praying in the spirit always equals activation.

Inspired Nugget

Don't forget that Jesus was the word made flesh and you are flesh being made into the word. At times, God is going to share with you his mind, eyes, and what he feels. I have seen and been in worship before and smelled a sweet-smelling fragrance. You are a spirit-being, so all these things God will open to you.

Touch. At times you may not see angels or demons in the spirit world, but you will feel things if you're spiritually sensitive enough. The Bible talks about Jesus being the high priest that can be touched by the feelings of our infirmities (Hebrews 4:15). So, things that Jesus feels at times, he will let you feel. Remember, Jesus is the word. At times you will feel other people's infirmities. You will feel other believers back pain or headaches when your discernment is working.

Inspired Nugget

This is the reason why it's important to be prayerful, humble, and rule your spirit and your emotions well. To really flow in discernment, you must be good at picking up people's issues but not letting them overtake you. At times, you will feel other people's sadness, but it's not time to be sad. The word is showing you these things so that you know how to pray and minister. The word knows the mind of the spirit and prays the mind of the spirit. Also, keep in mind that through the eyes of God, you will see other people's business. The word needs to trust you with people's personal stuff (Romans 8:27).

Taste. Have you ever wondered how, in a dream, you're able to taste things? Or how John the revelator could taste the word, even though he was in a vison or revelation? (Revelations 10:10). Remember, in the spirit you have other senses.

Smell. The same applies with smelling. There are many who testify that they can smell demons. I have personally never smelled a demon, but I have smelled the presence of God (1 Corinthians 12:17).

Hearing. At times, you will hear things through discernment. God primarily deals with me through my ear gate and my sense of touch when it comes to discernment. God wants every prophecy to be judged.

Sight. God, at times, will do what's called a 'Holy Spirit outline' over a person. This is when God is pointing that individual out for further ministry. Some people will see angels and demons. God will show you people's thoughts and intents (Hebrews 4:12).

So, think about this (Hebrews 4:12-13):

"The word of God is quick and powerful"

This means that the word in you is not only powerful, but alive! Have you ever wondered why when you do something wrong, the word will bother you late at night? Have you ever wondered how someone can talk about the word, and the thing that they discuss is exactly the thing you're struggling with?

"And sharper than any two-edged sword"

So, the word is very precise, like a surgeon's needle. Its job is to judge between, divide, and discern.

"Piercing even to the dividing asunder between soul and spirit and of the joints and marrow,"

So, true mature discernment can surgically divide between:

A. Spirit, which is your gifting, conscience, intuition.
B. Soul, which is your mind, will and emotions.
C. Flesh, (five natural senses) which is represented here by the bones and marrow.

At times, a person can prophecy but there is still no God in it. There is no anointing (Deuteronomy 18:20). A person can prophecy or say they discern things, but it's with the intuition and instinct. A person might speak a word of knowledge, but they have a fleshly motive. This is what the gift of discernment is for.

"And is a discerner of the thoughts and intents of the heart"

Words are spirits. Thoughts are spirits. When the devil came to Jesus, he didn't come in a suit and tie like in some movies. When the devil came to Eve, he didn't come as a giant two-legged beast with hairy legs and wings. The devil uses thoughts. *"Did God really say this?"* *"If you're the son of God, do this."* Discernment will help you discern the spirits behind the thoughts.

"And no creature is hidden from his sight"

Once again, words are spirits, emotions are spirit, and Jesus said the words that he speaks are spirit and life (John 6:63). Ask yourself, is anger a spirit or emotion? Is lust a spirit or an emotion? We have emotions, but we are not overcome by emotions. We are men and women who rule our spirit well.

Warnings About Discernment!

Now, brothers and sisters, I would be remiss if I didn't tell you that discernment is one of the most abused terms and abused gifts in the body of Christ. Here are some rules for discernment that will keep you out of trouble:

A. You must recognize the difference between discernment and intuition. Intuition relies on instinct; discernment relies on the spirit of God.
B. If God gives you to discern something, it will never be for gossip, tearing a person apart, for division, hatred, humiliation, variance or strife. You cannot

say you discern something that's gossip. God will punish you for that.

C. Even when you discern something negative, God will lead you to pray or restore, never to back bite. *"If a brother be overtaken in a fault, you who are spiritual, restore him"*. (Galatians 6:1)

D. Discernment has good peaceable fruit. If you think you discern something and it causes division or confusion, this is not from God. God hates things that divides brothers (Proverbs 6:19).

E. When you really operate in discernment, you must learn to keep things private and not gossip. God hates a talebearer (Proverbs 18:8, 20:19, 11:13).

F. Beware of people who use discernment for material gain. Some people have discernment strong enough to pick up your problems even though you never spoke a word. Watch for individuals who will exploit people simply by pointing out the problem. Remember, God doesn't give something and look to take it away. Just because a person has a gift doesn't mean they are right with God.

Another thing is that as you grow, you should discern more than demons. Immature discernment will discern only negative things and demons, but you have four classes of things you should discern:

A. God: You should be able to discern God and God's presence. If you can't discern that God lives in someone, then you are missing out.

B. Angelic Beings: You will, at times, be aware of the presence of angels, not just demons.

C. The Spirt of Man: This is what Hebrews 4:12 was all about. He said the word divides soul, spirit, and bones and marrow. When someone is giving a message or speaking, God will allow you to discern if they are speaking from their flesh or the spirit. This is one of the most vital uses for discernment. Also, this level of discernment is vital for the healing ministry. If God hasn't pointed out to you the infirmity, then how can you be accurate?

D. Demonic Powers: You will see demonic powers and even some things that you would rather not see. Just remember, if God is pointing them out, he's giving you power to deal with them. Never allow fear to overtake you.

Inspired Nugget

The Bible says in 1 Corinthians 11:29, *"for he that eateth and drinketh unworthily eateth and drinketh damnation on himself not discerning the Lord's body"*. Now brothers and sisters, we have already established that you are part of the Lord's body (1 Corinthians 12:12-13). I know that this scripture is typically used for communion, but is God's body in the crackers and juice or in the church? Do you believe God cares more for crackers and grape juice than he does his people? But we will reverence the type of shadow of his body rather than respect the God in one another. If you really want to discern something, learn first to discern and respect God's body and not a type and shadow of his body.

Or do you think He will let you honor the crackers, but hate and slander your brother? And we wonder why we are weak and sickly! It's because we haven't developed spiritually to see God's body yet! The scripture says that, *"if we would judge ourselves, we wouldn't get in trouble with God"* (1 Corinthians 11:31). I want to challenge every individual to take a month and ask God to help you discern things about yourself! I want to task every believer to ask God to search your heart! God, I want pure motives! *"Create in me a clean heart and renew a right spirit within me"* (Psalm 51:10).

The next step is seeing God the way God sees you. Once you have dealt with your own issues, I don't want you to go back to guilt. Hebrews 9:14 talks about your conscience being purged from dead works to serve the living God. You cannot serve God with a guilty conscience. Guilt hinders your flow. Don't be mistaken, God isn't asking you to do evil and ignore conscience, but to go through your sanctification process and not return to the things that make you guilty. When your conscience is clear and you're confident, then you can judge and discern spirits (1 Corinthians 10:4-6).

Just a recap:

*Discernment is not the same as intuition.

*Discernment is spiritual. Intuition is emotional and environmental.

*Discernment searches the hearts. Intuition is instinct.

*The prophet must never confuse discernment for intuition.

*The prophet may be touched by emotions and infirmities but must never allow emotions to rule them.

*A man or woman of God who doesn't rule their spirit well is like a city without walls. That means anything can come in and go out (Proverbs 25:28).

*True discernment never brings confusion.

*God won't allow you to discern things that will fill you with envy, hatred, division and strife.

*God hates things that sow discord among brethren.

*Can we pray today that God will give you discernment?

The Irritation

Now, there is a place in scripture that says this: *"And it came to pass as we went to prayer a certain damsel possessed with a spirit of divination, met us, which brought her masters much gain by soothsaying. The same followed Paul and us and cried saying, "these men are servants of the most high God which show unto us the way of salvation." And this she did many days. But Paul being grieved turned and said to the spirit. I command thee in the name of Jesus Christ to come out of her. And he came out that same hour."* -Acts 16:16-18

I want to point out to you the particular point in scripture where is says the spirit grieved Paul. Or a better translation would be annoyed or irritated. One of the first indications that your discernment is working is that certain speech or actions will irritate or disturb you. Again, you must separate this from your prejudices and intuition. Are you being annoyed because that's not your type of music, or your type of hobby? Are you being annoyed because that person doesn't share your brand of politics? You must remove your personal bias from the situation. When real demonic forces are speaking, if you have this gift, operating in it will really disturb you. An irritation or feeling grieved is one of the first levels of discernment. It should go like this:

1. The first level is irritation as we discussed. If demons are talking or a spirit is even near you, it should bother you. At times, it will become hard to ignore the individual.
2. Hearing is next. Usually when my discernment is kicking in strong enough, the Holy Spirit will have something to say or direct me.
3. Sight/Feeling: At this level you will begin to see things. You will see if people are demonic or holy simply by just looking at them. I can't explain how I know, but I just know. I have seen people and they have a glow to them. You will feel other people's infirmities at this point. You may feel their back pain or headache, pain or their sadness.
4. Thoughts: At times, God's thoughts will be shared with you. The scripture even discusses how God is a discerner of the thoughts (Hebrews 4:12, Matthew 9:9). God will reveal other people's evil thoughts to you. This is why you need true discernment and not intuition. Relying on intuition will cause you to assume and judge thoughts from experience.
5. Open Vision: At this level, God will open the spirit reel to you. You will see angels and demons. You will see clouds and shadows. Even though this level can be developed, it's usually prophets that are called to this level of discernment.

Again, we operate in mature and loving discernment. Our discernment is to help others and not to gossip about them or shun them. True discernment doesn't just see demons, but it looks at the hearts of men. True discernment sees God in other people. True discernment will help others overcome rather than abuse them. One of my biggest struggles as a new Christian had to deal with people with a false discernment. I have told people in prison, "You are a Christian, aren't you?" "You don't fit here; I see it all over you", and the conversation turns into ministry because they understand God hasn't forgotten them, opposed to, "You're a murderer! You're a thief! You are violent!" Even though I see it, telling them their faults doesn't always have value. Remember that just because you see something, it doesn't mean it's what God is saying in that hour.

Father, in the name of Jesus, we praise and thank you for your word today. God, we thank you for exceedingly precious promises. God, we lay aside every weight and sin that easily besets us. We repent from every evil motive. God, we come before you today touching and agreeing. We come together agreeing for activation in the spirit. God, give us discernment on today. You said you would pour out your spirit on all flesh and that we would see visions. And God, we declare today that we will be activated. God, we declare that we will walk worthy of the gift and vocation in which we are called. We will use this gift for you glory. In Jesus name, Amen.

Teachable Guide

Explain the gift of discerning of spirits.

What scriptures in the Bible promise that discerning of spirits?

Is the discerning of spirits an utterance gift or revelation gift?

Show me an example of the discerning of spirits.

How do you receive discerning of spirits?

What is the difference between an utterance gift and revelation gift?

What chapter in the Bible talks almost exclusively of discerning of spirits?

Where does the Bible list discerning of spirits?

If I operate in discerning of spirits, does that make me a prophet?

Can anyone ask for discerning of spirits?

8

The Word of Wisdom

"For to one is given by the spirit the word of wisdom"

-1 Corinthians 12:8

One day long ago, after I gave my life to Christ, I had a peculiar dream. In my dream I observed a blueprint. I realized at some point in the dream that the blueprint was a schematic from God. In my dream, I now had the plan on how to build a particular house. When I woke up, I noticed that at times when I would read the scriptures, things would outline to me or pop out like a pop-up book.

God was giving me wisdom and spiritual understanding of his word, but I was confused. I thought wisdom was counsel, or things that God reveals in the future tense, as some preachers say. I thought wisdom helped you understand mysteries. And then one day, it hit me. I was reading the Bible and this popped out to me. Ephesians 3:10 reads, *"To the intent that now unto the principalities and powers in heavenly places might be known by the church, the manifold wisdom of God."*

Now, this word 'manifold' doesn't just mean abundant, but multi-faceted. The word for wisdom in Greek is 'Sophia'. Wisdom is not just knowledge, but the application of Godly knowledge in your life. Wisdom will allow you to understand Gods language and his blueprint for kingdom. Now, you can have wisdom in a lot of areas. There is heavenly wisdom and there is earthly and demonic wisdom (James 3:13-18). The wisdom we want is heavenly wisdom with good fruits. Here are the many things the gift of the word of wisdom will allow you to do:

1. Wise counsel for future plans: Genesis 41:34-38
2. Wisdom to understand dreams and visions: Daniel 1:17, 2:14, Daniel 5:11-12, Ecclesiastes 8:1
3. Wisdom to understand scripture: 1 Corinthians 13:2, Revelations 13:18, Ephesians 1:17-18
4. Wisdom to lead: 1 Kings 3:9

We now see that the word of wisdom is a very multi-faceted and multi-purpose gift. Let's look at some examples. Most of the time people receive words of wisdom, it has to do with things in a future tense or counsel for a future plan.

Now, remember Jesus was the word made flesh (John 1:14). Now, you are flesh being made into the word (2 Corinthians 3:18). So, when you're talking about the word of wisdom, it's not just you repeating something wise. It's the living and breathing word of God manifesting himself to impart wisdom to the hearers. You must start seeing the gifts of God as the word activating in you. You must start seeing your mind as the mind of Christ.

A. It's the word of wisdom because you are speaking an inspired word.
B. It's the word of wisdom because it's a living breathing biblical principle and gift coming to life in you.
C. The word part is the living word.
D. The wisdom portion is God's thoughts. It's literally God sharing a portion of his wisdom with you, letting you see what God understands.

Counsel

Wisdom for counsel is not just treated as a luxury in the Bible, it's needed. Isaiah 11:3 talks about the spirit of counsel. Notice how, in scripture, wisdom has a very close synergy with prophecy. Daniel and Joseph interpreted dreams through the wisdom of God, but the interpretation ended up being something that God wanted to do in the earth. It wasn't just enough for the dream to be interpreted, there was a plan needed afterwards. Wise counsel is needed in the church to give a plan to what the prophet is seeing. Could you imagine the lives that would be lost if Joseph would have seen the famine, but didn't give a plan? Sometimes, we expect God to do our job for us when he's given us wisdom to accomplish a task.

Wisdom to Understand Dreams and Visions

Some people see interpreting dreams as a separate gift, but the truth of the matter is it comes with the word of wisdom. Remember, gifts of revelation are supernatural things revealed to the spirit of a man and his intellect. The Bible talks about how no one knows the things of a man better than the spirit of a man. Even so, no one knows the things of God like the spirit of God (1 Corinthians 1:10). This is why the answer and interpretation belong to God. You can read a million books or have a Ph.D in all kinds of fancy dream studies, but some mysteries will only be revealed through the spirit of God and the gift of word of wisdom is the key (Daniel 5:11-12, Daniel 2:21-23). Note here how the gift of wisdom and the gift of prophecy work together (Genesis 41:38-40).

The Difference Between Wisdom and Revelation

Now, if you will notice in the scriptures, Ephesians 1:17 talks about the spirit of wisdom and revelation in the knowledge of him. The scripture is very specific. It says there is an anointing of wisdom and revelation in the knowledge of him ('him' being Christ). These are two separate anointings in the spirit of God that we will break down. Keep in mind the word of wisdom is manifold. It's diverse and has a few uses. These twin anointings of wisdom and revelation have a few purposes. If you study the scriptures, you will discover that even ministering angels will bring an answer to you. The scripture says:

a. They are to open your eyes of understanding (verse 18). Your spiritual eyes are your eyes of understanding. Some people are gifted in the spirit but they can only move accidently in the spirit because their understanding of seed faith principles is limited. When your eyes are open, you know how to walk in principles. Therefore, teachers should have no problem ministering in the anointing because their eyes should be open.

b. That you may know the hope of his calling: to know and to have a peek at the amazing things that God has promised you. God will show it to you through wisdom and revelation.

c. The riches of the glory of his inheritance in the saints: again, what belongs to you and what God has invested in you. God didn't give you the anointing to live oppressed.

d. And the exceeding greatness of his power towards us who believe: this means through the eyes of understanding through wisdom, God will teach you how to walk in power.

Now, here is the difference between wisdom and revelation. Notice how, in Revelations 4, 6, and 7, God says come up here or come and see. The revelation portion is the vision that you will see. In Revelations 7:13, he sees a vision of the saints and the tribes that are called out. After the vision, it is explained to him what he just saw.

Sometimes, you will see things spiritually, or have a dream or vision, but you won't really understand what you have seen. When you don't understand, it's a call to prayer. The wisdom portion is when God explains it to you. Again, this is how wisdom and revelation work together. Wisdom unlocks prophetic things. A revelation with no explanation can be useless. Job 33:14 talks about how God speaks to men in one way or another, but man does not perceive it. It mentions how, at night, God seals his instructions. The wisdom of God, the blueprint of God, helps us understand the mind of God.

Wisdom To Understand Scripture

The Bible says that the natural man understands not the things of God because they are spiritually understood (1 Corinthians 2:14). When we are talking about the word of wisdom, we are talking about the mind of God and how God shares his thoughts with you. Verse 16 says you have the mind of Christ. Therefore, it's important for you to see yourself the way God sees you. For wisdom to operate, you must let God's mind and thoughts be in you (Philippians 2:5).

Armed with the mind of God, you will understand things that others don't get. It's not that you are smarter, or even more knowledgeable, but the way that the Holy Spirit operates here is to compare spiritual things with natural things (1 Corinthians 2:13). This is how God typically pours out the word of wisdom in teachers. So, as we can see, the word of wisdom is versatile depending on what your overall calling is. There are testimonies of people not even being able to read, but God gives them wisdom to teach the word like the way Jesus did.

The Eyes of Understanding

The Bible talks about the eyes of your understanding being enlightened. Now brothers and sisters, this is not a 3rd eye, like some in the world like to say, but this is seeing things through God's eyes. Your spiritual eyes are your eyes of understanding. The word of wisdom affects the way you perceive and understand things (Ephesians 1:17). This is the spirit of wisdom and revelation in the knowledge of him. This is the anointing of the word of wisdom. It's not there just to make you wise, but it's the spirit of wisdom AND revelation in the knowledge of him. This means that this wisdom is about the things of God. Let's join together today and pray as Paul did that you would receive the spirit of wisdom and revelation in the knowledge of him.

Wisdom To Lead

There will be times when you need counsel and wisdom to lead people. The word of wisdom is excellent for this role. Remember Solomon. He was just anointed king and leader over Israel. Instead of asking God for riches, he asked God for wisdom to lead the people.

1 Kings 3:5-13 talks about how Solomon asks for an understanding heart to judge the people. God gave Solomon all that he asked for and more. We need this wisdom in the church to make wise judgments and to lead God's people, wise understanding hearts that exercise in wisdom, and to have their eyes of understanding open. And remember, having wisdom is not about always having deeps insight or revelations. God will give you very practical wisdom for situations. If you notice in the following chapters, Solomon made very practical business decisions that made him successful.

Wisdom and the Prophetic

Wisdom and the gift of prophecy have a very close relationship. In fact, it's almost guaranteed that wherever you have true prophecy, it will contain elements of the word of wisdom and the word of knowledge. In this way, wisdom can be very predictive. But remember, there are different aspects to the word of wisdom. Prophecy, tongues, and interpretation are like the freeways, or open roads, that the other gifts can flow through.

Joseph was a great example of how the word of wisdom and prophecy are linked. Genesis 41:17-18 says this: *"And Pharaoh said unto Joseph, In my dream, behold, I stood upon the bank of the river: And, behold, there came up out of the river seven kine, fatfleshed and well favoured; and they fed in a meadow:"* Now, Pharaoh saw in a dream seven fat cows that represented seven good years of plenty, and seven thin cows that represented seven years of famine. The dream was prophetic, and the message was prophetic. It was a foretelling of events, but without the wisdom of God, the prophecy could not be unlocked or understood.

Another example is how Daniel interpreted the king's dream. The dream and the message were prophetic in nature, but it took the gift of the word of wisdom to unlock it. If prophecy is forth-telling, then the foretelling can't go forward if no one understands it. We read in 1 Corinthians 14 how important it is to edify the body through interpreting tongues. The same rules apply here.

This still happens today. Before the Covid pandemic, I received a dream about a coming storm. I automatically assumed that the dream was about my current events in my life when I should have sought God diligently for the answer. Some things will just come to you and other things you will need to seek God for. Daniel was a good example. Daniel would fast for an answer. This is why wisdom and prophecy are so closely related. Wisdom is to prophecy what interpretation is to tongues. We are seeing visions and having dreams and experiences, but the word of wisdom is the key component that will unlock things.

Also, remember that the word of wisdom is a gift of revelation. It's one of the mind gifts. We should be discerning on what we share with people and how we share it. Remember, Joseph's entire family understood his revelations and prophetic dreams, but hated him for it. Don't be so anxious to share everything with everyone that you see (Genesis 37:5). Once again, this is the reason that the word of wisdom and prophecy are almost inseparable. It's not just the ability to understand the prophetic, but the counsel that goes with it. After Joseph interpreted Pharaoh's dream, God gave him the wisdom for the strategy and then the leadership to carry it out.

What does the word of wisdom look and feel like?

Remember, there are a few ways God will express or reveal himself and the word of wisdom is no exception. Also, this is a spiritual gift. It is meant for us to ask God for wisdom. You won't be in the spirit 24 hours a day, 7 days a week. So, you must treat this gift as any other gift. When the anointing is on you, you will feel like you have an answer for anything. At times, God will speak and to the listening ears it will sound a lot like prophecy, but it's a word of wisdom.

1. Sometimes, when it comes to things like dreams, you will just know or understand the answer.
2. At times, you will read the Bible and the spirit of God will use the Holy Ghost to outline a passage to study. At times, things will pop-up like in a book.
3. You will have counsel for difficult situations and circumstances through the Holy Spirit.
4. The Holy Spirit will bring instant insight to visions and prophecies, even other people's visions.
5. The Holy Spirit will always compare spiritual things with natural things.
6. At times in prayer, you will receive ideas, revelations, wisdom and teachings.
7. In difficult situations, the Holy Spirit will bring things back to your remembrance for the situation, giving the appearance of wisdom.
8. Biblical concepts will come easily and gracefully for you. You will grasp things that others study hard for.
9. You will have a mouth of wisdom that at times is difficult for others to counter.
10. The wisdom of God will guide you towards being humble, kind, and meek (James 3:13).

11. God will often give you a word of wisdom through a dream.

How will I know what wisdom is from God?

Now, my friends, I must warn you there are a lot of false teachings and a lot of false prophets going around. I want you to beware of false teachers, false doctrines and evil wisdom. Here are some tips to help. Remember, a lot of the times when God speaks, he interrupts your thinking. There are times that I have been in devotional prayer, and after prayer in the quiet, a series of scriptures will come to my mind. As I begin to follow this thread, all kinds of revelation nuggets pop out. These are the thoughts of God. We think at times because the thoughts are not predicting the future that they are not God's thoughts. But the Holy Ghost is teaching us, comparing spiritual things with spiritual (1 Corinthians 2:13).

1. The companion gift to the word of wisdom is the gift of discerning of spirits. Ask God for discernment. At times, a person can be saying the right things but the spirit behind it is not a spirit from God.
2. Any spirit that doesn't glorify Christ, acknowledge his God head, or his manhood is not a spirit from God (1 John 4:1-3).
3. Any spirit or person that claims to have a secret exclusive revelation is not from God (2 Peter 1:20).
4. Any person or spirit who claims a revelation or knowledge that's glorifies selfish gains, lust or hatred is not from God (James 3:13-15).
5. Any wisdom that's selfish, earthly, sensual or demonic is not from the Lord.

6. The wisdom that is from God has good fruit. It's humble, easily entreated and peaceable. It doesn't try and make a name for itself. It recognizes the thoughts of God but still submits. The mind of Christ will teach you to serve (James 3:17, Philippians 2:5).

7. The Bible says that when the Holy Ghost is teaching, he compares spiritual things with spiritual. This simply means that he doesn't mix spiritual things with philosophy or mix carnal things with spiritual to gain understanding. I have seen some preachers say things that are unseemly or go off on a tangent because they tried to compare a lot of natural things to the spirit. Or even worse, get caught up in philosophy. Remember, the Holy Ghost wants to compare spiritual things with spiritual (1 Corinthians 2:9-16).

8. The Holy Ghost likes to show you through the word of wisdom, the things of God that are freely given to us.

I want to point out one more thing. The word of wisdom is a gift that is fed through prayer and study. Remember, we talked about seed faith principle. God can give you a raw gift, but the gift will only increase through nurturing the seed. Spending seedtime in prayer, fasting and study will elevate you. The first time I can remember God manifesting like this in my life was on a Daniel-fast as a young man. Now, God is always faithful to meet me in prayer, fasting, study or meditation. At times, as I pray in tongues, God will download teaching into me. Remember, get in the spirit; don't take the gift for granted, but exercise and grow it.

If you haven't noticed already, the word of wisdom deals with the mind of God in you. Just like we learned about discernment as your spiritual senses, the word of wisdom deals with your spiritual mind and your spiritual cognition (2 Corinthians 3:18). The Bible talks about how a wise man's eyes are in his head. The eyes from the word of wisdom are different from a prophetic eye or a discerning eye. Your spiritual eyes are your eyes of understanding (Ephesians 1:17-18).

One last warning for the word of wisdom: I want you to know as a teacher that the whole purpose of a teacher is to bring understanding. Wisdom always brings understanding. It's very easy to become deep and super spiritual, but not very relatable when an anointing of wisdom is on you. Don't forget, you can understand all mysteries and all knowledge yet still be unloving (1 Corinthians 13:2). It's very important that you have balance in your life. There is nothing like a person that can understand deep revelations but can't pay the light bill. Always know who you're teaching and what you are teaching. Some things will be too high for people and you'll lose them. The teacher must be very practical. Study how to be humble. One of my next books will be on the power of true humility. An abundance of revelations creates a wealth of knowledge, and knowledge can puff us up. But your job is to build-up the body of Christ.

Let's pray for activation:

Father, in the name of Jesus, we praise and thank you for your word today. God, we thank you for exceedingly precious promises. God, we lay aside every weight and sin that easily besets us. We repent from every evil motive.

God, we come before you today touching and agreeing. We come together agreeing for activation in the spirit. God give us the word of wisdom. You even said in your word if we lacked wisdom we could ask not doubting. You said you would pour out your spirit on all flesh and that we would see visions. And God, we declare today that we will be activated. God, we declare that we will walk worthy of the gift and vocation in which we are called. GOD, WE WILL USE THIS GIFT OF WORD OF WISDOM FOR YOUR GLORY AND TO EDIFY YOUR PEOPLE. In Jesus' name we pray, amen.

Teachable Guide

Explain the word of wisdom.

What scriptures in the Bible promise word of wisdom?

Word of wisdom: an utterance gift or revelation gift?

Show me an example of word of wisdom.

How do you receive word of wisdom?

What is the difference between an utterance gift and revelation gift?

What chapter in the Bible talks about word of wisdom?

Where does the Bible list word of wisdom?

If I operate in word of wisdom, does that make me a prophet?

Can anyone ask for word of wisdom?

9

Introduction to the Gifts of Power:

Gifts of Healings

It was about 1997. I was a young man still living in my father's house. Now I don't know why, but for some reason I woke up that morning with a really bad pain in my foot. I don't know if I injured it while running, or twisted it, or jammed it, but it was really bothering me. And then I remembered what I had heard about in the scriptures. I remembered how the Bible said speak to the mountain. In that moment, I had this idea to speak to my foot. I opened my mouth and began to rebuke the pain in Jesus' name. Suddenly, my pain went away. I was so mesmerized that I stomped on the foot. I jumped up and down on it. Anything to see if I was really healed. I was blown away by the power of God! This was one of my first experiences with the gifts of healings.

So, if you have noticed, this is one of the nine gifts of the spirit that's plural. It's plural because there are several ways and quite a few areas that God works in healing. The gifts of power are not about the communication of God, or the mind or God, but the demonstration of God's power. When you receive healing as a gift, it's defined as a supernatural healing that goes beyond the laws of nature and physics and that cannot be replicated by modern medicine. Miracles and faith also operate in this manner. If it could be achieved naturally and with little or no effort, then it would not be a miracle. Here is more on healing. And by the way, I don't advocate that anyone would call their ministry a healing ministry. God can heal through anyone who will believe.

A. It is by the stripes of Jesus that we are healed. Now, if anyone has ever researched the passion of Christ, they will tell you with certainty that the Romans would frequently use 39 stripes to punish people. The reason for this is because the scourging was tested and known to kill a man with 40 lashes. The Romans tortured a man all the way until the last stripe. In the ancient world, sickness and disease was broken up into 39 specific categories. The point is there is a healing stripe for every condition, malady and issue.

B. The biggest thing that God wants you to know about healing is that God wants to heal you. He wants you to be healed. He sent his son to die for your healing. Why wouldn't he want you healed? Let's not make excuses for God, claiming that he just wants us sick for his glory, or thinking that it makes us deeper and religious to accept sickness.

C. You need faith to be healed.

D. No matter whose faith is working, faith always works. Most of the time, you must figure out how God wants to heal you. Will you get healed because of someone else's faith? Will you get healed after instructions are followed?

E. Salvation is connected to healing. When God heals you, he saves you. When God saves you, he heals you. The two are linked. James 5:15 lets us know how the prayer of faith will heal the sick, and if he's committed any sins, they will be forgiven. When God heals you, he saves you, and when he saves you, he heals you. The provision was made for our healing.

The 39 stripes are significant. In the ancient world, diseases were broken down into exactly 39 categories. It's these categories, or stripes, that the Lord will normally allow a person to specialize in. Just like, in the natural, you have doctors that specialize in children's medicine, back pain, internal medicine, brain surgery and I can go on and on, the gifts of healing operate in the same manner. God can use anyone to heal, but some anointings are specialized. With this being said, some people testify about how God will heal back pain for them, or people from wheelchairs with no problem, but it may require something else for deafness or blindness. This doesn't mean that it's impossible for God to heal, but the instructions are important. You will find that your healing anointing has an affinity for a certain condition.

Now it's important to understand not just if God will heal you, but how God heals:

- A. God will heal through the laying of on hands by elders, praying a prayer of faith (James 5:14).
- B. God will heal you through the power of agreement.
- C. God will heal you through your confession of faith.
- D. God will heal you through somebody that is gifted in the gifts of healings.

In this instance, we are talking about someone gifted. As we dive deeper into the gifts, God wants you to understand the synergy of all the gifts. Remember, the question is never if God wants to heal you or not. The question is how God wants to do it.

If you can remember in the Bible, there was a story about a man named Naaman the leper. He was a great man from Syria in 2 Kings 5:1. He suffered from leprosy but when he heard that the God of Israel could heal, he went there. The man of God, Elisha, told him to bathe in the Jordan seven times to receive his healing. Now, how would this man receive instructions for healing if Elisha couldn't hear from God?

What about Jesus making clay from spit and putting it on a blind man's eyes? Remember, faith comes by hearing, and hearing by the word of God. You don't gain faith only by hearing the written word, but by the spoken or prophetic word. This is why it's important to grow your spiritual eyes and ears. The word and knowledge and discerning of spirits work in concert with the gifts of healings in order to fulfill God's will. The word of wisdom will give you instructions on what to do to receive healing.

How do I receive the gifts of healings?

First off, like we mentioned before, if you have a burning desire for this gift, it's very likely that God put it there. If you desire to be activated in this gift, agree with me right now for God to do it:

Father in the name of Jesus, we praise and thank you for your word today. God, we thank you for exceedingly precious promises. God, we lay aside every weight and sin that easily besets us. We repent from every evil motive. God, we come before you today touching and agreeing. We come together agreeing for activation in the spirit. God, give us the gifts of healings. You even said in your word that by your stripes I'm healed. God, we declare today that we will be activated. God, we declare that we will walk

worthy of the gift and vocation in which we are called.
God, we pray the prayer of faith that you would imbue us
with your healing power and virtue. We choose to believe
your word on today. In Jesus' name, amen.

How do I walk in the gifts of healings?

You must hear God's instructions and God's voice to walk effectively in this gift. You must know how God will heal. Does God want you to speak to the sickness or lay hands? Did God give you instructions on what to do? You must understand that the will of God is not automatic. Even though God wants his people saved and healed, you must believe it to receive it. Remember, Hebrews 5:14 talks about having your senses exercised. Sometimes, you will perceive or discern through the Holy Ghost.

What if the person does not get healed?

Remember, it's always God's will that you be healed. So, if a person is not healed right away, ask for instructions. Sometimes, the person must follow instructions. Sometimes, God wants them to be healed through persistent faith confession. The bottom line is that if we make excuses for God in healing us, we will never truly operate in faith. Don't make excuses if you don't see healing come the first time. Keep knocking, keep persisting, keep believing.

It's the will of God to heal us, just like it's the will of God to save us. But the will of God is not automatic. God wants to partner with us in the earth to complete his will. Thy kingdom come, thy will be done on earth, as it is in heaven. Remember this about faith. No matter whose faith it is, faith works.

If you pray over a handkerchief, and another believes that God will heal them from the handkerchief, then God will do it. Remember, like the woman with the issue of blood, faith will pull a healing from God. Without faith you can do nothing. If you believe in God, all things are possible.

Is casting out devils the gift of healing?

No. The reason I say this is because there is infirmity, and then there is a spirit or demon of infirmity. There is sickness, and then there are demons of sickness. Yes, at times you will need to deal with a spirit of infirmity, but casting out devils is a promise to the believer, not a separate gift (Luke 14:11, Mark 16:17). The gift of discerning of spirits will help you in this area.

The Laying-On of Hands

The laying-on of hands is significant because the exercise signals impartation. The laying-on of hands and healing are closely connected. Now, sometimes Jesus just spoke, but most of the time he laid hands on people. In fact, there are no instances in the Bible where Jesus cast out a devil with the laying-on of hands. When he casted out devils, he spoke. When he prayed for healing, he either laid hands or spoke. This is one of the ways that the scriptures promised us we would heal in his name: *"They shall lay hands on the sick and they shall recover"* (Mark 16:18).

Remember, when operating in the gifts of healings, it's important to know how God wants to heal. Does he want you to lay hands? Does he say 'speak to the sickness'? Did he say to put mud on their eyes? Therefore, it's important to hear God's instructions clearly.

Why don't some people get healed?

People who don't believe in spiritual gifts will often cite negative circumstances in order to try and prove a point that God doesn't heal anymore. The bottom line is that, even in the Bible, there were certain circumstances in which Jesus could not work healing and miracles. Matthew 15:38 shows us that a lack of miracles and power is usually because of a lack of faith or unbelief. But there are also other reasons that some don't get healed. Remember, the will of God is not automatic. Does God want us all saved? Yes. Is every man and woman saved? The answer is no. It's the same with healing. Let's examine some reasons that stop the gift of healing from flowing.

1. **Unbelief**. The bottom line is that if there is no faith, God cannot operate. Remember, faith is the substance of things hoped for! Faith is heaven's currency! Faith is how transactions are made in heaven. Without faith, it is impossible to please God. If you are praying and laboring for someone to be healed, the first thing you should do is build their faith. And faith comes by hearing, and hearing by the word of God.

2. **No seed in the ground**. Remember, Matthew 17:20 says, *"if you have faith as a grain of mustard seed"*. Again, what do you do with seed? You plant it! Jesus always likens the kingdom to seed (Matthew 13:31). Remember, we talked in another place about sowing into the flesh and sowing into the spirit. A lot of people know the mechanics of faith. They know they should confess and they know they should believe, but they are too lazy to put works to their faith. James 2:14 talks about putting works to

your faith. When you are spending time in prayer, again, you are sowing into the spirit. A farmer doesn't wait until there is a drought and a need to finally sow. The farmer sows in advance knowing that he will need the harvest. Remember, if you have faith as a seed, then you can say unto the mountain 'be ye removed and cast into the sea'. Our mountains don't move at times because we have forgotten that having a seed is part of the faith process (Hebrews 11:6, Galatians 6:7). There is an old bedtime story about an ant and a grasshopper. If you remember the story, the grasshopper played all summer when things were going well while the ants labored. After a while, the summer turned to fall and then winter, and the grasshopper began to be in need while the ants enjoyed what they stored up. When you're tempted to be lazy, just remember the ant and the grasshopper.

3. **Lack of agreement/contention**. Remember, James 4 talks about where wars and fights come from. For example, you have one person refusing to take a vaccination shot because they feel like it's not faith. You have another group of church members who despise the first person for not taking a shot. You have another group that's using a covid crisis to grandstand. How can God move in such contention? How can God move in an environment of bickering and fighting? Jesus said if two or more agree concerning anything, it shall be done for them. But we slander and look down on not only the world but our brothers and sisters in Christ! What good is it if we build a ministry but build it at our brother's expense?! And why do we need to tear down

ministry to build our own? This lack of holiness is one of the primary reasons that God won't hear from heaven and heal our land.

4. **Lack of Godly patience**. James 5:7 tells us that we should be like farmers or husbandmen and wait patiently. A farmer not only knows what he has planted, but how long some things take. If the conditions are not right, a good farmer will prepare the ground. He will remove every weed, rock and tree that will hinder his seed's growing. He constantly waters it and nurtures it until it blooms. He kills off pests that would plague it. This is the same with preparing the heart for healing. You may have faith, but you may have to labor with someone in faith until they believe for their healing. We get impatient and treat the things of God like microwave snacks. Furthermore, we fail to realize that the scripture says you will have what you sayeth! That means plural or more than one time! So many times, you must confess something once, twice, or even a few times. You must not stray away from persistent faith. Patience is the perfect counterpart for faith. Patience doesn't mean just sitting there but persistent active patience. I'm talking about the kind of patience that's confident and works the process. Remember, those that come to God must believe that he is and believe that he is a rewarder of them that diligently seek him.

5. **Lack of compassion**. If you noticed, nearly every time Jesus healed or did a miracle, he showed mercy and compassion. Just take Matthew 17:15 for instance. A woman asks Jesus to have mercy on her son because he's a lunatic. Jesus' response to the

call for mercy is healing and deliverance. We don't see some healing and miracles because we have stopped caring like Jesus did. We have become a self-centered social club church rather than laboring in prayer and fasting until a healing or miracle is accomplished. The enemy in this generation distracts us with the cares of this world. We are distracted by our family problems, our jobs and our love lives. I pray over this book that God will give us wisdom and divine strategies in our lives to gain control over petty issues so that we can get back to walking in power.

Teachable Guide

Explain the gifts of healings.

What scriptures in the Bible promise gifts of healings?

Is gifts of healings an utterance gift or revelation gift?

Show me an example in the Bible of gifts of healings.

How do you receive gifts of healings?

What is the difference between a power gift and revelation gift?

What chapter in the Bible talks about the promise of healing?

Where does the Bible list gifts of healings?

If I operate in gifts of healings, does that make me a prophet?

10

The Working of Miracles

"Notwithstanding lest we should offend them go thou to the sea and cast a hook and take up the fish that first cometh up; and when thou hast opened its mouth, thou shalt find a piece of money: that take and give unto them for me and thee". -Matthew 17:27

Now, we have read the story before about how the Lord gave instructions for a miracle. But what if Peter had wavered? What if he would've half-followed instructions, or didn't follow them at all? In this chapter, we will discuss the working, or miracles, and even give some testimonies about miracles. But first of all, what is a miracle? Put simply:

A. A miracle is something supernaturally that God does that defies the laws of physics and nature.
B. A miracle can be so improbable that it can only be defined as God's providence. For instance, a fish with a coin in its mouth doesn't defy nature, but the fact that God set it up is impossible according to natural means.

So, the gift is called the working of miracles. 1 Corinthians 12:29 says, *"Are all apostles? Are all prophets? Are all teachers? Are all workers of miracles?"* Now the reason the gift is called the working of miracles is because the miracle must be worked. God will give specific instructions as to how he wants the miracle to be completed. God is looking for someone who will follow instructions completely.

Moses is another great example. God worked amazing miracles through him, like parting the red sea and causing it to rain mana on the earth. But Moses allowed the people the aggravate him. God told Moses to speak to the rock and water will come out. Numbers 20:7 talks about how God was very specific on how he wanted the miracle to be worked. But instead of speaking to the rock, Moses said this: *"Hear now ye rebels must we fetch you water out of this rock?"* And the Bible says Moses struck the rock rather than speaking to it. Moses made a few mistakes here that are very detrimental when it comes to operating in the working of miracles or any gift for that matter:

A. He used his gift in frustration, rather than operating in love.
B. He took credit for the miracle when boasting about bringing water from the rock for them.
C. He failed to follow instructions.
D. He did not show God respect before the people. (Numbers 20:12)

My brothers and sisters, I want you to know that the Bible says that to him whom much is given, much is required (Luke 12:48). People assume that God is a God of puppy love and that he is never angry. But I know God to be a killer! Both Moses and Aaron suffered dire consequences for their actions. Moses had his assignment cut short and never entered the Promised Land. Aaron died earlier than expected. If we are going operate in the power of God, we must show him reverence and respect. Never touch God's glory by accepting the worship of others.

Never Accept Worship!

Notice how everything that God made that's spirit likes worship. Demons like worship. The devil himself likes worship. And men especially like worship. If you are going to operate in the working of miracles, I want you to be careful of allowing people to worship you. Remember, you are a spirit. It feels good when people say, "you're a great preacher" or "you're better than all of the rest". Moses was a perfect example. The enemy's desire is that your assignment is cut short. He wants you to never make it to your promised land.

How do I receive the working of miracles?

Remember, like any other gift, to ask in faith not doubting. Ask and it shall be given, seek and you shall find, knock and it shall be opened unto you. Remember, all these gifts are gifts! I don't want you to see one as harder to operate in than the other. I want you to ask not wavering. If God has put the desire in you to ask, then it's likely waiting for you.

How do I operate in the working of miracles?

You follow God's instructions. Remember, the miracle must be worked. You must have clear communication with God on the matter. Remember Moses stretching out his staff over the Red Sea? Or Jesus telling Peter to cast his net? You must obey what God gives you to do. Therefore, it's important to hear God and have your spiritual ears awakened. How would Moses know to stretch out his staff if he couldn't hear God? How would Peter know how to get the great catch if he never heard Jesus?

Let's touch and agree if you really desire this gift:

Father in the name of Jesus, we praise and thank you for your word today. God, we thank you for exceedingly precious promises. God, we lay aside every weight and sin that easily besets us. We repent from every evil motive. God, we come before you today touching and agreeing. We come together agreeing for activation in the spirit. God, give us the working of miracles. You even said in your word that all things are possible to them that believe. God, we declare today that we will be activated. God, we declare that we will walk worthy of the gift and vocation in which we are called.

Different Kinds of Miracles

Now, the working of miracles can be very diverse and cover a lot of ground, but there are several categories of miracles that God can and will do. They are typically broken down into a few areas:

A. Provisional Miracles: Remember, miracles will always show God's sovereignty over the physical laws of science. A provisional miracle is when God bends the laws of nature just for your provision. Yes, God will defy the laws of nature just to make sure you're taken care of. An example of a provisional miracle would be turning two fish and five loaves into enough food to feed 5,000 people (Matthew 14:13-21). Another good example would be the woman with the jar of oil (2 Kings 4:1). Again, a man of God followed heaven's instructions and worked the miracle. God is concerned about even the most basic of provisions for us.

B. Physical Miracle: This is what we often call a miracle healing. There is healing, and then there is miracle healing. A healing would be a fever leaving or pain going away. A miracle healing or physical miracle is when entire limbs grow back. Being raised from the dead is not a healing, but it most certainly is a physical miracle.

C. Geophysical Miracle: This is when God totally and completely upends the laws of science and nature. This could include walking on water (Matthew 14:22). A geophysical miracle can be getting temporarily raptured from one place to another (Acts 8:39), or even parting the Red Sea (Exodus 14:21).

So, God is still the God of miracles. The Bible says that if you have faith as a grain of mustard seed, you can say unto this mountain be ye removed, and cast into the sea (Matthew 17:20-21). And nothing shall be impossible for you. There are testimonies of God growing legs and arms back. If you obey God in working the miracle, then nothing is impossible.

Interview with Overseer Davidson

I was fortunate enough to sit down for an interview with Overseer Davidson, who currently oversees things at Cornerstone Family and Worship Church in Las Vegas, Nevada. Overseer Davidson has participated in mission work and has seen many things and miracles in her life.

Minister Moreland: Hello Overseer Davidson. Can you tell the readers about who you are and what you do?

Overseer Davidson: I'm Overseer Davidson and I oversee things here at Cornerstone Family and Worship Church.

Minister Moreland: Overseer Davidson, can you testify about miracles you have seen?

Overseer Davidson: Where do you want me to start?

Minister Moreland: The other day, God was dealing with me about miracles of provision, like with the two fish and five loaves.

Overseer Davidson: I remember one time as a child, I was supposed to go on a church trip, but I didn't have the funds. They kept asking for the money and I told them I'll have it. After a collection of the money, God provided me not only with what I needed but more than I needed to sustain me on the trip. That's one.

Minister Moreland: WOW! In this book I'm explaining the gift called the working of miracles and how important it is to hear God to work the miracle.

Overseer Davidson: It's very important to hear the voice of God. You must hear God speaking and that it's not you acting out of yourself. You've got to know that you're one whom he hears when you talk to him. You just have to know your place in him. The miracles work that way when you dedicate yourself diligently. And during a time when there is a need, then the miracles and the wonders, they work together.

Minister Moreland: So, part of the working of miracles is the need?

Overseer Davidson: Is the need, right. If there is a need and a compassion too. Because when Jesus took the two fish and five loaves, he had compassion on them and he didn't want to send them away. He didn't want to send them back hungry, so he sat them down and performed that miracle. The same way in this day and time, God has a compassion. Sometimes, we have things that we want and desire, and God says if you're one that will diligently seek him, he'll give you the desires of your heart. So sometimes, miracles can come that way and you probably just forgot about it, or it's not the main thing on your plate. But God is mindful of us. Sometimes, he will do things for us that is our heart's desire and we don't even know how it happened. All we know is that there was a desire and that thing happened.

Minister Moreland: What is the connection between obedience and operation in the gifts?

Overseer Davidson: Obedience is very important. You cannot operate in the true gift unless you're obedient.

Minister Moreland: I talk a lot about how it's important to be under somebody and have integrity. I talk about how many people have just went and started their own thing and don't feel like they have anyone that they will be under. I explain the need for obedience. And not just the obedience of hearing God, but obedience to leadership.

Overseer Davidson: The thing about it is that you have to put in your book that they understand that God has a divine order. Jesus was under the leadership of the Father. He was subject to the Father. That's why God came in the form of a son.

Minister Moreland: I had a Holy Ghost experience recently even as I was studying about provisional miracles and God being a provider. I felt the anointing and I felt a miracle in my belly. Can a miracle be released into someone else? Do healing and miracles have to be released?

Overseer Davidson: It depends on what the situation is and what God wants to do. Because sometimes, it's right there like the man at the pool of Bethesda. But it's always about God's word doing it, and God's word has to meet you where you're at. When God's word comes and meets you where you're at, you've got to accept his word for who he is. And if you don't accept it, you can't receive a miracle, even though you have a miracle there in front of you.

Minister Moreland: That's what I was saying. I was talking to someone recently and explaining that very concept to them. The person told me, "When you started speaking to me about it, I heard God say get up and praise him", and they didn't do it. My question was, "Your miracle was right there. Why didn't you do it?"

Overseer Davidson: Sometimes it works like that! And he'll tell you to go on the way. Some things have to be done right then and there! You have an example of one who Jesus told him to go wash in the pool and he would be healed, and then you had one blind Bartimaeus who was healed immediately. It depends on the situation and the circumstance that you're in.

Minister Moreland: So, there is a power in obedience?

Overseer Davidson: Obedience is a big key over everything! Obedience is better than sacrifice. Whatever you do, be obedient!

Minister Moreland: Yes ma'am. Thank you, Overseer Davidson.

What's the difference between the working of miracles and the gift of faith?

Now remember, a miracle must be worked, but faith must be spoken. God can work a miracle in two ways:

A. The gift of faith. This is a gift of supernatural faith where God gives you to speak something in order to create a miraculous outcome. Most of the times that miracles are activated is because of the gift of faith. As we will discuss later, faith involves confession. So, if the miracle or miracle healing was spoken, it's the gift of faith in operation.

B. The working of miracles. This means that, rather than the miracles just being spoken, it had to be worked. This means that very specific instructions need to be followed. Did God say stretch out your hand over the Red Sea? That was a miracle. Did God tell you speak to the winds and the sea? That's the gift of faith in operation. At times, and in certain situations, all three power gifts can become activated. If someone is raised from the dead, that will often require a miracle and a healing. Is someone missing arms, legs and eyes? It may require all the power gifts.

I cannot stress enough how important it is to hear God's instructions clearly. We are missing out on miracles because we haven't allowed our spiritual ears to be quickened and brought to life. Faith comes by hearing, and hearing by the word of God.

Teachable Guide

Explain the working of miracles.

What scriptures in the Bible promise miracles?

Can you name three types of miracles?

Show me an example in the Bible of the working of miracles.

How do you receive the working of miracles?

What is the difference between a power gift and revelation gift?

What chapter in the Bible talks about the promise of miracles?

Where does the Bible list the working of miracles?

Can anyone ask for working of miracles?

11

The Gift of Faith

"Now faith is the substance of things hoped for the evidence of things not seen" -Hebrews 11:1

"To another faith by the same spirit" -1 Corinthians 12:9

Now to understand the gift of faith, you first must understand that there are different kinds of faith. The Bible describes quite a few different types of faith. The Bible talks about how every man has been given a measure of faith. Romans 12:3 shows us that faith is measurable, and everyone has been given a certain level of faith. Here are different types of faith the Bible talks about:

A. Saving Faith: The faith that saves you in Jesus Christ (Romans 10:8-9)
B. Little Faith: Matthew 8:26
C. Systematic Faith: As we have discussed in previous chapters, concerning mustard seed, seed time and harvest.
D. Prophetic Faith: God will allow you to operate in your gift in proportion to your faith.
E. Most Holy Faith: Jude 1:20. This is the faith that allows the word and the spirit to pray for you, even when you don't know what to pray for.
F. The Gift of Faith: This is a supernatural level of faith that is given to accomplish the impossible. In this chapter, we will discuss the gift of faith.

The gift of faith is a supernatural faith that is given by God to do the impossible and miraculous. People who operate in this level of faith are usually radical and world-changing. The gift of faith is, more often than not, behind most miracles and healing. There is a portion of scripture where Jesus says this: *"Have faith in God"* (Mark 11:22), but the correct translation in Greek is, *"Have the faith from God"*. So, this altogether is a different level of faith than simple saving faith. This is the kind of faith that comes directly from God. This is the God-type of faith.

But what is faith?

The scripture says this: *"Now faith is the substance of things hoped for, the evidence of things not seen."* (Hebrews 11:1), but many people still struggle to understand this interpretation or meaning. I have had the best success explaining it in the amplified version of the Bible: *"Now faith is the assurance (title deed, confirmation) of things hoped for (divinely guaranteed), and the evidence of things not seen [the conviction of their reality—faith comprehends as fact what cannot be experienced by the physical senses]."*

So, let's explain this piece by piece:

A. *Now faith*: I know it's a play on words, but I want you to fully understand that to really operate in faith, and the gift of faith, then it must be a 'now' situation. You're expecting God to do it NOW! If you had to wait until next week, then it would not be faith. Even when you cannot see it immediately, you have an expectation that it's done now!

B. *Is the assurance (title deed confirmation)*: When you buy a house or a car, unless you have loads of money sitting around, do you normally pay for the house in cash? You would normally put down some confirmation or surety of payment and then you would have access to the house or car based on your payment confirmation! (I believe God that one day soon I will be able to purchase my home with cash only, but I'm using an analogy). This means you get to drive the car around or live in it, even though you did not pay it off. You must look at faith as the way business is transacted in the spirit. Faith and covenant are the currencies. You get access to all of heaven when you deposit your faith. Therefore, without a deposit (faith), it is impossible to please God. You must look at faith as God's currency!

C. *Of things hoped for (divinely guaranteed)*: Faith is the currency deed, and confirmation of the divinely guaranteed. You must understand that, just like in a natural sense. When you buy a product, most of the time they will give you a warranty. This certifies that the product works. The reason they do this is because the company's name is attached to the product. God is the same way. He wants you to know that real faith is divinely guaranteed because you are believing in HIM, and his name is in your mouth.

D. *And the evidence of things not seen [the conviction of their reality—faith comprehends as fact what cannot be experienced by the physical senses]*. Faith comprehends things as facts that are not visible! You must understand that people who operate in this level of faith will seem odd because they believe the invisible. They believe in things that they cannot see or promises that seem impossible.

How do I receive the gift of faith?

Remember, like all the other gifts, if you want it, you must ask God not doubting and not wavering. But with this gift, you must not only ask, but hear the word because faith comes by hearing, and hearing by the word of God (Romans 10:17).

Let's pray that God will activate you in faith:

Father in the name of Jesus, we praise and thank you for your word today. God, we thank you for exceedingly precious promises. God, we lay aside every weight and sin that easily besets us. We repent from every evil motive. God, we come before you today touching and agreeing. We come together agreeing for activation in the spirit. God, give us the gift of supernatural faith. You even said in your word that nothing is impossible to them that believe. God, we declare today that we will be activated. God, we declare that we will walk worthy of the gift and vocation in which we are called. God, we pray the prayer of faith that you would increase our faith. We choose to believe your word on today. In Jesus' name, amen.

When you release your faith, whether it's stopping the rain or mending bones, you must speak faith. The Bible talks about how you believe what you have spoken (2 Corinthians 4:13). If you believe that God can mend bones, then you must speak it. The gift of faith is not passive, but assertive, disruptive, and won't take no for an answer. Here is a little more on the gift of faith:

A. The gift of faith doesn't always wait for a season or a word. Believing in the word of God is enough. The gift of faith moves the hand of God. Remember the woman with the issue of blood. The gift of faith causes disruptive miracles and blessings.

B. You cannot be negative and have the gift of faith. You can't believe something and speak against it.

C. The gift of faith is the catalyst for many miracles signs and wonders, even in the modern era. It's just like prophecy to the word of knowledge. It's one of the primary gifts behind the scenes that are causing things to activate.

D. Faith is the currency, deed, or confirmation that allows access to things unseen. It draws spiritual principles and Godly power into natural realms and not only attracts but moves the hand of God!

E. Remember, no matter whose faith is active, faith works.

F. God will speak to people with the gift of faith to do impossible or awkward things. For instance, telling Moses to speak to the rock, or telling you to speak to the winds and sea.

G. People with the gift of faith also seem odd because they hope against hope. They walk by faith and not by sight.

H. Remember, if you can already see it, then it's not faith and you're not operating in the gift of faith. The gift of faith isn't operating in an assured outcome. You don't need the gift of faith to know that your job's paycheck is coming in a week.

I want to encourage you to have the faith of God, to have the God-type of faith and see where God takes you.

Teachable Guide

Explain the gift of faith.

What scriptures in the Bible promise the gift of faith?

Can you name three types of faith?

Show me an example in the Bible of the gift of faith.

How do you receive the gift of faith?

What is the difference between a power gift and revelation gift?

What chapter in the Bible talks about the promise of the gift of faith?

Where does the Bible list the gift of faith?

Can anyone ask for the gift of faith?

12

Introduction to Motivational Gifts:

Prophecy and Teaching

It was sometime in 2018. A homeless man approached the church and requested money for a bus ticket and food. A fellow minister, who I will call Minister K, went with me on the drive. Soon after, I dropped the man off, gave him bus money and made sure he had something to eat. Minister K and I both saw things differently. Minister K couldn't understand, for the love of God, why I would go out of my way and waste resources on a man who had no intention of serving Jesus. I could not understand how Minister K could be so heartless and uncaring. It wasn't my responsibility to know what he was doing with the money, and somehow, I could not help but feel compassion for the man. We agreed to disagree and I quickly realized that we were both right with different insights, and that we showed two different demonstrations of motivational gifts!

In this section, we will be introduced to the motivational gifts. Remember, there are gifts of manifestation, which you can readily ask for. Then there are gifts that are motivational gifts. The last set of gifts are offices. But what are motivational gifts? Motivational gifts are, what I would like call, 'personality gifts'. The gifts go beyond something that you can ask for. It's something that you are born with. It's part of your personality. They are part of your make-up. They are called motivational gifts because they are what the Holy Spirit uses to motivate you.

When I was younger, in church, there was a lot of talk discussing your calling. Apostle Davidson taught us at a very young age that when you're seeking to learn what you're called to do, you can find your answer in your personality. Teachers, for instance, are very seldom exhorters. Exhorters very seldomly store up useless bits of information like teachers. Can an exhorter learn to teach? Yes, but a teacher is born with the call, personality and gifting to teach. Can a teacher learn to exhort or give? Yes, but it comes naturally for someone with the gift of exhortation.

When I first began to teach the scriptures, I learned who I was because I was encouraged to speak as a preacher. I realized very quickly that I didn't feel comfortable as a traditional preacher. I knew I had gifts, but something didn't feel right. Therefore, it's of the utmost importance for leaders to not only discern demons, but to understand intents and destiny. The gift of discernment is not only to see evil things, but to discern gifts and callings. You will never be able to step fully into your calling and gifts if you cannot honor the place of other people's giftings.

For instance, some people place too much emphasis on preaching, so they never allow a teaching ministry to flow in their church. And others make the same mistakes with evangelism, mercy, serving, exhorting, prophecy, and nearly every call. The scripture clearly states: *"If the whole body were and eye, where were the hearing? If the whole body were hearing where were the smelling?"* (1 Corinthians 12:17). The Bible also says: *"And the eye can't say to the hand, I have no need of thee: nor again the head to the feet, I have no need of you"* (1 Corinthians 12:21)

Remember, this isn't just about manifestation gifts, but also personalities and callings. So, I hope that in this section you will find yourself. The scripture we are using is Romans 12:6-8.

Prophecy and Teaching

Now remember, we dealt with an entire chapter concerning prophecy and the importance of prophesying according to our faith. But the amazing thing about prophecy is that it can be an office, a calling and a motivational gift. I want you to remember the story I told you at the beginning of the chapter. The motivational gifts are not just about your abilities, but about how you see things. We don't want to focus so much of the supernatural demonstration of prophecy, but the passion and desire to speak as if they are God's oracle. The gift is about proclaiming the word of God and being motivated to proclaim it, rather than seeing a vision.

Now, you don't have to tell the future or walk in the word of knowledge to speak under inspiration. The word of God itself is inspirational. This is why I often scratch my head at those who claim that God doesn't speak today. I'd like to ask each one of them if God used their pastor or spoke through them. The bottom line is that there is a manifestation of prophecy, and then there is a motivation to speak under inspiration. Never make the mistake of thinking that just because a person isn't seeing the future of having prophetic dreams, that God isn't using them. Here are some facts about the motivational gift of prophecy.

Remember also, you're going to operate according to your faith. Your entire development will be determined by your faith. We are also going to talk about some of the traps and cons of each gift. These are not just titles but personality traits. So, it's very important to understand the pitfalls of each gift. You can also have more than one. If you haven't guessed buy now, my motivational gifts are teaching and mercy. Not every gift looks spiritual, but don't let your eyes deceive you. These gifts are given by God and are necessary for a healthy church.

A. People with this gift are preachers and speak with fire and passion.
B. Just because you have a motivation to speak God's word, it doesn't make you a prophet.
C. You can have the manifestation gift of prophecy but are not a very good speaker. Moses was a good example.
D. This gift motivates you to speak God's word. There will be a burning desire to preach.
E. You're going to have a person that's very fired up, zealous and motivated so it's very important to give them good teaching.
F. A person with this gift will have a specific focus of preaching the word of God. It might even take them some effort to slow down and teach or explain.

Cons of the prophecy motivational gift:

A. They can become impatient with teaching.
B. They can become proud of their speaking abilities.
C. Dynamic preachers are flashy and sought after, so this can be a snare.
D. They can be tempted into thinking they don't need other parts of the body because of the ease and success of preaching.

E. They often equate the ability to speak with the ability to lead or pastor. This can cause them to step into arenas God didn't call them to.

Remember our chapter on integrity and stay humble. Never allow success to cause you to falter.

Teaching

I'll never forget when I was a young man, around 21 years of age. I had just received Jesus as my Lord and Savior. My pastor at that time was a middle-aged holiness pastor. One day in bible study, the pastor just so happened to declare that Allah was another name for God. It irritated me so much that I spoke up and politely mentioned to him that Allah was the name of a different God. The pastor was extremely annoyed that some young kid who had just barely gotten saved would dare to correct him. After some back and forth and huffing about him knowing better and being the pastor, I shut up, but I couldn't let it go. I didn't understand why, but it really irritated me that someone could get things wrong concerning the word of God in this manner. By the next bible study, I had studied on the name and came armed with facts. Needless to say, that pastor was not pleased with me at all. I had all the traits of a teacher then and I didn't even know it.

The teacher covers two areas. There is the ministry office of teacher, and then there is the motivational gift of a teacher. The teacher's job is simple: his number one job is to bring understanding. When you read the scriptures, it talks about how Jesus opened their understanding of the scriptures (Luke 24:45). You must remember that the gift is the Jesus part of you. Remember, an eye cannot say to a hand I don't need you. You are part of his body. So, just like he opened the scriptures, it's the teacher's job to open the scriptures. A person with the motivational gift to teach will have a burning desire to teach the word. Here are some other personality traits of a teacher:

A. This personality trait is a real stickler for God's word and truth.
B. This is someone who stores up information and facts that others would consider useless.
C. There is a passion for accuracy. This motivates them to heavily research.
D. These individuals are very technical. They want to not only understand concepts, but they want to pick them apart and see how and why they work.
E. A lack of reverence for truth and scripture can really anger or annoy them.
F. They want to teach everyone.

Here are some cons to the teaching motivational gift:

A. Instead of being proud of their speaking prowess, they can be proud of their knowledge.
B. They want to teach everyone a lesson, even when they are wrong.
C. Since they are technical, they will often pick apart another person's message rather than hear them.
D. They can often become condescending when other preachers don't seem to know certain facts.
E. They can load up their message with a lot of useless information, which can make them boring.
F. They can be tempted to stifle the flow and energy of a service when coming behind someone energetic rather than flowing in it.
G. Because of the abundance of knowledge, they can overestimate their importance.

Remember, these gifts are motivational and not about a title or an office. These gifts are what your ministry focus is about. They determine how you view things. They are parts of your personality. It's the Holy Spirit's job to lead you, but even in leading you, he has given you a personality and made that part of you a gift to others.

Teachable Guide

Explain the motivational gift of prophecy or proclaiming.

Explain the motivational gift of teaching.

Can you name three personality traits for a person with the motivational gift of prophecy?

Can you name three personality traits for a person with the motivational gift of teaching?

What are some pitfalls if you have a motivation gift of prophecy or proclaiming?

What is the difference between a motivational gift and a manifestation gift?

What chapter in the Bible talks about motivational gifts?

Where does the Bible list the gift of faith?

Can you change your motivational gift?

13

Serving and Exhortation

Now, some may not understand or see serving as very spiritual. They will dismiss it as something unnecessary. But even the scripture says *"let him who is greatest among you become your servant"* (Matthew 23:11), and, *"serving is also part of the mind of Christ"* (Philippians 2:7). So, the motivational gift of ministry or serving is of utmost importance in the body of Christ. In fact, the spirit or heart of a servant is really captured in Philippians 2:5-7. Here are some facts about the gift for serving or ministry.

Some of us have the title of a minister, but certain people with this gift to serve take it to another level. These are the people that you see staying at the church for long hours. These are the people that you can call at the midnight hour to help perform a task. If they see a floor that needs to be vacuumed or a church bathroom that's dirty, they will clean it without hesitation. They don't clean things or do tasks so that later they can bring it up or score points. A person without the gift of serving can be quick to remind you about all the things that they did. A person with the gift to serve will just do it because it's in them. Where teachers give their information, and givers give money, servers give their time and effort.

These are the people that make the church run. They are like the life-blood of the church that allows events and ministry to flow freely. They free up teachers, prophets and pastors to focus on the word of God instead of cleaning the church or serving tables. In fact, there is a passage of scripture in Acts that mentions this very thing. In Acts 13:1, it talks about this very thing. They choose deacons, men that serve and full of the Holy Spirit, to handle matters of business. If you are a pastor or a church leader and you are dealing with individuals who have trouble being faithful, instead of getting angry, consider a person for the job with the gift to serve. I know that there are many with the title of minister and that is, by definition, a call to serve, but some people have the true gift of serving.

Inspired Nugget

I want to add something before the next section. If you ever really read the 2nd and 3rd chapters of Genesis, you will learn valuable truths about Adam. If you will notice, God told Adam to tend to the garden and keep it. God told Adam to name every animal. He gave him a lot of work to do but Adam did not complain. In fact, the Bible hints that he had fellowship with God. But when Adam was kicked out of the garden, he had less work to do, yet God told him he would work by the sweat of his brow. Adam now only had the job of tilling the land and providing for his family, but it was hard.

Which is a more demanding task; farming the land for your family, or naming every animal on earth? Which is more difficult; tending a garden and protecting it when it's hundreds or maybe thousands of miles wide? Or only farming to feed the family? The answer is clear: Adam had less work outside of the garden, but now it was difficult. The difference? When Adam was in the garden, he could walk with God in the cool of the day. When he was out of the garden, he lost fellowship. When Adam was in the garden, he spoke over things. He declared things. Outside of the garden, he only had his flesh to help him.

If you believe you have a gift to serve and you are burned-out or discouraged, I want to encourage you through this book on today. I'm praying that you will rekindle your passion to serve by walking with God. The power to serve comes from the Holy Spirit. In our flesh, we can only do so much. When you are truly serving and walking with God, the hard tasks seem easy. When you're serving because of fleshly reasons or to be seen, the easy tasks are now hard. Re-ignite your passion and your desire to serve today. I declare your gift of serving and your heart will be whole, in Jesus' name! Your church needs you. God has partnered with you to serve in the earth and tend to the garden and keep it. Stand up and be the servant that God called you to be.

A. A person with the gift to serve truly knows how to serve with humility.
B. This individual doesn't serve to make a reputation for themselves.
C. This person doesn't serve out of self-doubt or a low self-esteem, but out of a sincere passion.
D. This person values loyalty, dedication and obedience.
E. This personality trait will become frustrated with others who see something needs to be done but won't do it.
F. Tasks that seem tiring and exhausting to others will seem routine to the person who serves.
G. This individual doesn't like to be in the spotlight very much.

H. This individual can get passionate and aggressive when the person they are serving is verbally attacked.

Here are some cons to the personality trait and the gift of serving:

A. Whereas a prophet or pro-claimer is proud of their speaking, and a teacher is proud of their knowledge, a server can become proud of their works.
B. A server can be so passionate about wanting to serve and help that they can be exploited by people.
C. A server sometimes needs a person in their life to encourage them to rest. True servers can be tireless, leading to issues and burnout.
D. Servers can get into marriage trouble if things are not properly communicated, or the server is spending an inappropriate time serving the church rather than putting time and energy into a marriage.
E. A server can be tempted to feel like they are not important.

Exhortation

If a server likes to give of himself, the exhorter is nearly consumed by making others better. The word 'exhort', by definition, means to encourage. But using just encouragement doesn't tell the entire story for the exhorter. You know these people because they are always trying to coach you through the smallest matters. The exhorter is the person who will go to great lengths to make sure you are the best you. The exhorter will find things in you that you didn't know were there. The exhorter really doesn't care much for a pity-party and won't leave you to wallow in self-pity or a bad attitude. The exhorter does more than preach; they are trying to get you to your destiny.

A preacher and an exhorter are two different things. The preacher can speak well, but the exhorter will become your life coach if you let them. The exhorter doesn't stop because they are out of the pulpit. They are going to keep pulling and pulling at you until you come up a little higher. In fact, it can be annoying to hang with an exhorter at times because they won't let you make excuses. I had a time in my life when I was really down, and frankly, I did not want to be up. I didn't want to be encouraged and had a big pity-party for myself. I found it difficult to hang around exhorters that constantly suggested that I needed to become healed and whole. There are people called to a ministry of exhortation.

Exhortation and Prophecy

You must also realize that exhortation and the manifestation gift of prophecy have a very close relationship. This is because exhortation is one of the core reasons for the gift of prophecy. Remember when we read about the gift of prophecy, we discovered that exhortation was inherent in the gift. Again, 1 Corinthians 14:3 reveals that he who prophesies speaks edification, exhortation and comfort. These two gifts fit together like a hand and glove. So, a person can start off only exhorting, but the gift of prophecy will stir up in them. Or a person can start out prophesying and they will begin to exhort. The reason for this is because exhorting brings out the best in a person and bringing out the best lines up with God's word.

Acts 15:32 also confirms that there is a close relationship between the gift of exhortation and the manifestation gift of prophecy. We are talking about the passion to exhort. The motivation. Anyone can exhort, but some people are specially gifted in this. Here are some hints and personality traits for exhortation:

A. An exhorter is annoyed with pity parties and excuses.
B. An exhorter always sees destiny in you.
C. An exhorter is not afraid to tell you that you're wrong or in a slump.
D. People with a ministry of exhortation also step into the prophetic.
E. Exhorters won't give up on you easily. They want you to be your best.
F. Exhorters are always upbeat and optimistic.

Cons to an exhorter personality:

A. An exhorter can take pride in helping you get to a goal or take credit.
B. Exhorters are go-getters and sometimes don't care for details like teachers.
C. Exhorters must be told at times when to let people go.
D. Exhorters can become frustrated with mediocrity.

Teachable Guide

Explain the motivational gift of exhortation.

Explain the motivational gift of serving.

Can you name three personality traits for a person with the motivational gift of serving?

Can you name three personality traits for a person with the motivational gift of exhortation?

What are some pitfalls if you have a motivation gift of exhortation?

What is the difference between a motivational gift and a calling or office?

What chapter in the Bible talks about exhortation?

14

Giving, Ruling and Mercy

Like serving, there are many people in the body of Christ who may not consider giving a gift, or even very spiritual, but I can assure you giving is a gift. Paul mentions the gift in 1 Corinthians 13:3 when he says, *"And thou I bestow all of my goods to feed the poor."* He lists this gift of giving right after mentioning the gifts of prophecy and knowledge. But what is a gift of giving? The motivational gift of giving is a motivation or passion and desire to give to others for the growth of the kingdom.

Givers are normally very good with money and very frugal. Just like it takes faith to walk in the word of knowledge, it takes faith to give. People with the gift of giving usually go above and beyond what a normal individual would give. I knew a woman at one time who gave her only car to the church. A person with a true gift of giving will usually be good at accumulating wealth. They are good businesspeople and never turn down an opportunity to bless the kingdom. Givers will even give all their substance away at once if they believe that God is in it. Here are some traits of people with the motivational gift of giving:

A. People with the gift of giving are normally excellent with money and finances.
B. People with the gift of giving don't like waste and mismanagement.
C. The wealth is funneled to take care of kingdom business. A true giver is never broke.

D. Not only will they give money, but they will give material things like clothing, cars, or even the shirt on their backs.
E. God uses people like this to supernaturally fund kingdom work.

Cons to the motivational gift of giving.

A. They can desire to control ministry through giving donations.
B. They can be easily distracted by carnal things.
C. They can get comfortable in their money and forget God.
D. If they are not careful, they can become prideful and take glory for kingdom work.

Note that the Bible says that you are to give with simplicity. This simply means that there should be no strings attached or hidden motivations when you give.

Ruling

When dealing with ruling, we will separate them into two parts. There is a motivation gift of leadership, and then there is administration. People can be great leaders but lack the organizational skills of an administrator, and vice-versa. You can have a person that's a great organizer but a poor leader. In 1 Corinthians 12:28, it mentions gifts of administrations. So, we will treat them as two separate things.

The gift to rule, or what we would call in modern terms leadership, is the motivational gift to stand up and lead. Leadership takes the initiative to go forward. This person doesn't just lead by position but cultivates a healthy respect from others by making sound leadership decisions. Really good leaders start out as the best disciples. If you want examples, you must look no farther than Elijah and Elisha (1 Kings). The younger prophet served under Elijah until the very last moment that his master was taken away. There is a spiritual principle in being a good follower before you can be a good leader. Many people try and skip steps and never learn to follow. They then scratch their heads when they become leaders of people who won't follow. You will reap what you sow. If you desire to become a great leader, learn to follow first.

Great leaders are also good at properly using their personnel. A great leader will carefully examine the gifts and talents of others. If a person has the motivational gift of leadership, they don't have to throw around their title as a leader. The Bible says your gift will make room for you (Proverbs 18:16). Leadership is a learned trait but some people are born with it. People with this gift excel at everything that they do. If they are playing basketball, then they want to excel at it. If they play golf, then they are in it to win. They don't have to try intentionally to stand out from the crowd; it happens supernaturally. Here are some personality traits of a person with the motivational gift of leading. Also remember that the Bible says that you must lead with diligence. You cannot be a slacker and be a successful leader.

A. They desire to excel at whatever they do.
B. They are good at seeing various talents in others and spend time considering how to use them.
C. They have a low tolerance for foolishness and dysfunction.

D. Something about them and their attitude cultivates and commands respect.
E. They push for personal excellence.
F. They are fair and will never ask you to do work that they won't do.
G. They admit mistakes and take responsibility for them.
H. They have a good work ethic.
I. People follow their example of work and team-building over their title.
J. Good natural leaders become emotionally invested in their subordinates.

Cons to the leadership personality trait:

A. They can seem cold and less tolerant than givers or people with mercy.
B. They have very little patience for foolishness.
C. They can get proud in their leadership skills.
D. They can have a heavy burden for the people they lead.

Administration

The second part is a person with a gift of administration. A person with this gift and talent is extremely organized and will run a tight ship. Administrators are usually also good at finance and planning. All administrators are not good leaders. To be a leader requires a certain level of patience. Administrators are not motivated by leading, they are motivated by getting the job done. These are the people that you want over your finance department or counting the money box. Here are some things that will tell you if you have a gift of administration:

A. Administrators are extremely tidy and organized.
B. Administrators are nit-picky about rules and regulations in the same way that teachers are picky about the Bible.
C. Administrators are really annoyed at sloppy and unprofessional business practices.
D. Administrators will examine the level of organization in your church.
E. They are usually professionals in other fields outside of church.

Cons of the administrative personality traits:

A. They are usually not very good at outreach and street ministry.
B. They have a lot less patience than the person with mercy.
C. They are organized but don't always make great leaders.
D. They can seem aloof at times and distant, but they are actually in their head figuring out something.

Mercy

Mercy is a motivation gift that is needed more and more in the body of Christ. The gift of mercy will feed people when they are hungry. It will house them and even give the shirt off its back. Mercy differs from the gift of giving in that givers normally have something to give to support the kingdom. People with the gift of mercy will at times be in a state of lack themselves and still give.

The Bible says: *"Blessed are the merciful, for they shall obtain mercy."* (Matthew 5:7). There is a spiritual law at play here. God blesses the merciful with supernatural favor in situations because they have showed mercy to his people. The key is like the Bible says; to show mercy with cheerfulness. I have learned over the years that if you are going to show mercy to a person, and then complain about it, you forfeit your blessing. This is what the Bible means when God says don't let your right hand know what your left hand is doing (Matthew 6:5). It's very important that, if you're going to bless a person with a place to live, to not make a scene and cry about it. If you give a person in need $100, then don't complain. The power is not only in the obedience, but in doing it with cheerfulness. Here are some personality traits of a person with the motivational gift of mercy:

A. They have compassion on people that even others seem to give up on.
B. They give time, money and resources even when they don't have much to give.
C. They give a lot of 2nd chance opportunities.
D. They have big hearts for people.
E. They make good outreach material.

Cons:

A. They can give without considering their spouses or home life.
B. They can get in a habit of putting other's needs over their family's needs.
C. They can be bad at finances because their compassion gives too many chances.
D. They have such a big heart for people that they can seem naive at times.
E. They don't always make good leaders because of their easy-going nature.

15

Living Waters Exercises and Flows

The Rivers of Water

To understand these exercises, you must understand that the Holy Ghost flows in streams or rivers. The Bible said that out of you would flow RIVERS of living water. There is more than one river coming from the same source. Each gift, anointing, or office is its own flow or river (Psalms 1:3, John 4:10, 7:38). Prophecy is a river. The discerning of spirits is a river. Healing is a river. If you will learn how to step into the river or stream, then God will use you in it.

Inspired Nugget

I pondered how to explain these spiritual principles to people that are not initiated. One of the ways God showed me was a Firestick. A Firestick is a popular device that attaches to most televisions that allows for the streaming of movies and other digital media. We will look at the gifts like apps on the Firestick. I wondered once before how some people would enjoy additional apps on their Firestick, and in some cases find a limitless number of things to watch.

Every Firestick comes with apps preloaded, but some apps must be downloaded (prayer). Every app is its own unique service with different requirements. One app I downloaded even came in a bundle with TV. The main source was the internet behind the Firestick (the Holy Ghost). Without the internet, there is no stream. The

Firestick cannot find its purpose and potential without a network. The Holy Spirit is the person and the agent that allows you to log into God's network (the spirit realm). No matter who you are, you must understand that ultimately, it's the Holy Ghost that allows you to have access or not. The Holy Spirit is like your ISP or cable provider. Once upon time, I remember struggling with my Firestick, trying to figure out how to get certain features and apps to work. All apps are free to download, but there is a cost associated with it. I hope this section will help you understand how to step into some things. Here are the different rivers and how to enter.

The River of the Prophetic

Now, there are several ways to step into prophecy legally. Here we will discuss exercises on how to grow in these areas. I want to note that I've known people who God deals with when at rest. Rest is a big component.

1. Worship
2. Tongues and interpretation

Worship

Worship will nearly always attract God's attention. If you study the scriptures, you will discover that God is seeking someone to worship him in the spirit and in truth (John 4:24). Now, many of us know how to worship, but we don't know how to enter the spirit through worship. We don't understand that a very high worship will not only invite God in, but God will begin to take over the worship and give you the songs he wants you to sing. My old apostle used to call it 'catching the wave of the spirit'.

There is a difference between singing an anointed song, and then singing the song God wants to sing at that time. When God begins to take over and direct the music, it cannot be duplicated. It may go one way this Sunday, and another next Sunday. When you are allowing God to direct you like this, this is a great exercise in a prophetic atmosphere.

In this type of atmosphere, if one has exercised or built up their ear to hear, God will begin to speak. There are many rivers that can flow in this kind of environment. Everything from healing to discernment, every gift will be quickened but you must have an ear to hear. There was a time months ago when I heard a worship song in my head. I didn't really know all the words to the song, but I quickly found it and played it. As I began to worship, the hand of God came upon me. If you sing the songs God wants to sing, it will take you into the heavens.

More tips on prophecy:

1. Prophecy comes in waves. There is a rhythm to it.
2. True prophecy usually addresses the church.
3. When a person is prophesying, the Holy Ghost speaks more sternly.
4. The gift of prophecy is for the church. You'll never begin to prophecy in the mall, grocery store, etc.
5. Again, prophecy comes in a rhythm. The word 'Nabi' means to bubble up. Prophecy is inspired speech. If a person needs to think on what to say, it's not prophecy (Matthew 10:19).
6. Because prophecy is bubbling up when the person begins to speak, there is a rhythm and flow to it. It's a little different when interpreting tongues, but more on that later.

7. Some prophets function more like seers; instead of the prophecy bubbling up, they will see pictures.

Use worship, not just as an experience, but as a spiritual exercise. As you exercise, listen for the song that God wants to sing. Listen for the moving of the spirit. Different people move in different ways. Like we said in previous chapters, you must find your trigger. The amazing thing is if the river flows into the room, then whoever has that gift can ride the wave. Other prophetic people will know. When the spirit is flowing, listen. Practice listening in private prayer or worship. The more you do in private, the stronger your ear will be.

The River of Tongues and Interpretation

Now, we have discussed before how togues and interpretation work together. I want you to see it here as an exercise. Remember, God is the one who determines if you enter in or not. So, don't be discouraged if he doesn't speak. Here are three steps that will help you exercise in the interpretation of tongues. Now remember, you can exercise this gift if a person is speaking in another tongue, or if you're speaking. Exercising in private will prepare you to exercise in public. If another person is speaking, skip the first one and just listen.

1. Exercise speaking in tongues.
2. Exercise listening for the move of God.
3. Exercise speaking what He has given you.

The interesting thing about interpretation on tongues is there are a few outcomes and several gifts mentioned in the previous chapters associated with it. When God is using you to prophecy through the gift of interpretation, it will be with a lot of authority. When the word of knowledge speaks, it's informative and revelatory. When the gift of prophecy is speaking, it's God using you like a microphone. The sensation can be overwhelming. Remember, the interpretation you get can be:

1. Revelations from the word of wisdom, or instructive wisdom. If you need to recall what this feels like, read the chapter on the word of wisdom.
2. Revelations from the discerning of spirits. I will just begin to speak in tongues spontaneously and God will warn me about something.
3. Revelations from the word of knowledge. Again, read on word of knowledge.
4. Prophecy, as discussed before.
5. Teaching doctrine.
6. The answer can be musical or lead into worship.

As you grow in this gift, you will learn how to trust the prompting from the Lord on when to speak in tongues. I had an incident about a year ago, where I was driving and the Holy Ghost prompted me to call a person. When I called them, I started to hear tongues. As I spoke the tongues that I heard, the Holy Spirit then said, "Interpret!" very sternly. I opened my mouth to speak and a flow of the prophetic came out.

Now, I'm not telling this to boast or to receive glory. There is a lesson involved here. I heard the tongues, and as I began to speak, the flow started. It's just like in Acts the 2nd chapter. Many times you will hear the sound before the Holy Spirit blows like a mighty wind. If you're going to walk in the gift of interpretation of tongues, you must speak the tongues as God is prompting you. To be clear, I don't hear the tongues audibly, I hear them in my head in my thoughts. And when I spoke, God moved.

Exercises for the Word of Knowledge

We already went over what the word of knowledge is in a previous chapter, but did you know that the gift can be sharpened? Try this exercise:

1. Find a preacher that you trust and watch or record him ministering.
2. Make sure you pray first and ask for God to open your eyes or activate you. We never have operation without praying for activation.
3. Make sure that you don't know the answers or that you don't know what the preacher will say. If the word of knowledge is active in you, some things will come to you before the preacher even speaks it! Oh, the wonderful works of God! You will be amazed to find out that you are sensitive to the spirit of God, you just weren't paying attention.

When the word of knowledge is in the room, if you're sensitive when the preacher picks up something, you will also see it. Remember, you not only have rivers, but gates. Your eyes are gates, your ears are gates, even your mind is a gate (1 Corinthians 2:16). You must become a student of how God deals with you. The hardest people to teach are people that already have prophetic gifts because they may have a gift for prophecy, but don't understand or are not sensitive to revelational gifts. Get around other people that flow and watch them. Study if the word of knowledge comes to you in passing thoughts or pictures. Find the place of your sensitivity. I have had many times that I was sitting in church and I picked up something but ignored it.

Exercises for the Word of Wisdom

The word of wisdom is similar, but the key here is that the word of wisdom is instructive while the word of knowledge is informative. The word of wisdom is instructive (Ecclesiastes 10:10). If you can find someone that flows in wisdom, watch them as they move. You might see the answer before they speak. I have never known someone to flow in wisdom and understanding but won't study the word. The word and prayer feeds wisdom. Like I mentioned before, at times, things will jump out of the Bible at you.

1. The word of wisdom will come in revelated word.
2. The word of wisdom will give a solution to a problem.
3. The word of wisdom will give counsel and solve problems.

So, a good exercise is when you get in prayer for interpretation of a dream. Remember, when you have a dream or something you don't understand, it's a call to prayer. You're asking God for the anointing of the word of wisdom, or the spirit of wisdom and revelation (Ephesians 1:17). When you receive the answer, it will come in your thoughts. It will be like an epiphany. Usually when God gives the answer, he will seal it with his presence and his anointing so that he can bear witness to the answer.

The Discerning of Spirits

This one is very similar to the word of knowledge, only it involves more of your senses. Try going out on an outreach run one day.

1. Pray before you go out.
2. Go to places where you engage people.
3. Talk to people and shake their hands.
4. What did you pick up when you made contact?
5. Did you know the person was a Christian, or was burdened with devils even before they spoke?

Discernment is not about being aloof, deep and spiritual. Discernment is about helping people or warning you of danger. If you don't like to interact with people, you'll never grow in discernment. Remember, you must find that place of sensitivity. I had a guest come to my church some time ago. When the person came in the door, and I looked at them, the word "Apostle" came to my mind, but I ignored it. Moments later, this person was introduced as an apostle. It's little things like this that grows your sensitivity to impression.

The Power Gifts

Most of the time, when you operate in power gifts, it's because you have become adept at revelational gifts. So, if you want to learn about healing or miracles, seek God for revelational gifts. The word of wisdom will instruct you in a miracle. Discernment will help you diagnose a problem.

Thank you for reading this book. Thanks to all the ministers and leaders who inspired and supported me. A special thanks again to Pastor Latina Reagan who has ignited faith in me. Thank you, Apostle Albert Davidson and Pastor Aron Davidson. Thank you, Pastor Tom Scarcella for all your amazing insights and helping me grow. A special shout-out to Doctor Matthew Stevenson, who is also an inspiration. Most of all, I'd like to dedicate this book to Overseer Davidson, who has been a true spiritual mother to me over the years. Thank you!

www.ingramcontent.com/pod-product-compliance
Lightning Source LLC
Chambersburg PA
CBHW021636120626
46545CB00002B/563